Looked after children and offending

Looked after children and offending
Reducing risk and promoting resilience

Gillian Schofield, Laura Biggart,
Emma Ward, Victoria Scaife,
Jane Dodsworth, Alice Haynes,
and Birgit Larsson

Published by British Association
for Adoption & Fostering
(BAAF)
Saffron House
3rd Floor, 6–10 Kirby Street
London EC1N 8TS
www.baaf.org.uk

Charity registration 275689 (England and Wales)
and SC039337 (Scotland)

British Library Cataloguing in Publication Data
A catalogue record for this book is available
from the British Library

ISBN 978 1 910039 04 5

Project management by Shaila Shah, Publisher, BAAF
Designed by Helen Joubert Associates
Typeset by Avon DataSet Ltd, Bidford on Avon
Printed in Great Britain by TJ International
Trade distribution by Turnaround Publisher Services,
Unit 3, Olympia Trading Estate, Coburg Road,
London N22 6TZ

BAAF is the leading UK-wide membership
organisation for all those concerned with
adoption, fostering and child care issues.

Contents

List of tables

List of figures

Acknowledgements

We would like to thank the Big Lottery for funding this research on looked after children and offending as a partnership between the Centre for Research on Children and Families at the University of East Anglia and The Adolescent and Children's Trust (TACT).

We would also like to thank the many people who gave generously of their time to assist us in this project: service managers and practitioners who completed our questionnaires and attended our focus groups; staff in children's services and youth offending services who assisted us by contacting young people and supporting their participation in this research; the stakeholder group of experts who supported us throughout the project; and Voice and the young people's reference group who worked with us so enthusiastically.

But most of all we would like to express our gratitude to the 100 young people who agreed to share with us their thoughts and feelings about their often very difficult lives. We hope to have done justice to their stories and that the project will contribute to improving services and outcomes for young people, as they would wish.

Notes about the authors

The authors are all members of the Centre for Research on Children and Families at the University of East Anglia (UEA).

Gillian Schofield is a Professor of Child and Family Social Work. She has researched and published widely on the welfare of looked after children. She has a particular interest in attachment and resilience and with Mary Beek has recently published *The Secure Base model: Promoting attachment and resilience in foster care and adoption* (BAAF, 2014).

Laura Biggart is a Lecturer in Social Science Research Methods and Psychology. Her research focuses on social cognition and emotional intelligence, particularly in applied settings such as work-life balance and youth offending. Her current research is an ESRC-funded project examining emotional intelligence in social work.

Emma Ward is a Senior Research Associate. She has worked on a wide range of adoption, foster care and residential care research projects, focusing on the outcomes and experiences for young people, but also the perspectives of foster carers, adoptive parents and birth parents.

Victoria Scaife is a Senior Lecturer in Psychology. Her research interests focus on social-cognitive models of decision-making in populations of young people, particularly in relation to drug and alcohol use. She has recently conducted an assessment of support for the health needs of young offenders.

Jane Dodsworth is a Lecturer in Social Work. She has researched and published on a range of child welfare topics, including the analysis of serious case reviews. Her main research interest is in child sexual exploitation and she is currently undertaking a BASPCAN-funded research study exploring routes into it.

Alice Haynes was a Senior Research Associate at UEA and is now a Policy and Research Analyst at the NSPCC. She has conducted research on asylum-seeking and refugee mothers in England and has research interests in migration, identity, gender, child protection and fathering.

Birgit Larsson is a Senior Research Associate. Her current research is on young women and restorative justice, but she has also been involved in research on serious case reviews, neglect and residential care. She was previously a restorative justice practitioner, mediator and facilitator for a conflict resolution group in New York.

Voices of looked after children

I wasn't a good child because my birth family never showed me any love . . . I was always angry, all the time. And then my foster mother saw what was going on and she knew. So she gave me love and she gave me what every mother should give their daughter and I changed my ways and now I don't do drugs or anything bad like that. (16, non-offender)

Even if you are put in care, you can still have a good life, turn your life around, get grades and do what you want to do. Why risk it all for nothing? (18, non-offender)

I had this big thing, getting into trouble, wanting to beat people up and I thought I only want to beat this person up because I want her to feel the pain that I felt. Then I went to jail and my foster carer didn't want me. (17, offender)

I never really cared about anybody apart from myself – that was me when I was little. I didn't care about nobody . . . Because I didn't think anybody cared about me. I had been moved about so many times, it doesn't make you feel wanted does it, being moved around? (18, offender)

1 Introduction

There have been long-standing concerns about the risk of offending for children in care. Although a small minority of looked after children aged 10–17 offend in any one year (7.9%), this is more than twice the rate of children in the community (3%) (Department for Education, 2011). But also of concern in relation to serious outcomes is the fact that between a quarter and a half of children in custody are or have been looked after (HM Inspectorate of Prisons/Youth Justice Board (YJB), 2009). Among adult prisoners, it is estimated that 27 per cent have been looked after at some time (Social Exclusion Unit, 2002). There are also concerns that children in care may be inappropriately criminalised, with police involvement and charges brought for behaviour while in foster or residential care that would not have led to involvement in the youth justice system for children in their own families.

In response to these concerns, the *Looked After Children and Offending* project was funded by the Big Lottery Research Programme (2010–12). It was a partnership between the Centre for Research on Children and Families at the University of East Anglia (UEA) and The Adolescent and Children's Trust (TACT). The study investigated the characteristics and pathways of looked after children and the risk and protective factors that may reduce the risk of offending and promote resilience.

The project was designed to contribute to improving the life chances of looked after children at risk of offending and criminalisation and had the following research aims:

- to identify the risk and protective factors that increase or decrease the likelihood of offending by young people in care;
- to identify the resilience factors that can be promoted in looked after children to reduce the likelihood of offending;
- to identify features of the care and justice systems that may

1

increase/reduce the likelihood of offending and the criminalisation of looked after children;

- to identify the key transitional/turning points that are opportunities for interventions to divert children in care from offending;
- to make recommendations for policy and practice.

Almost all children in care are from backgrounds of deprivation, poor parenting, abuse and neglect, factors that together create risk for a range of emotional, social and behavioural difficulties, including anti-social and offending behaviour. However, repairing harm and promoting resilience through high quality care can occur at all stages in a child's development, including adolescence, thus providing windows of opportunity for change.

The multidisciplinary research team from UEA used a multi-level, multi-method approach to this study and carried out the following:

- a review of the policy and research literature;
- a survey in England and Wales of practice in local authority services for looked after children (LAC) and youth offending services (YOS);
- file searches and interviews in four diverse local authorities, with a sample of a) looked after young people who had been in contact with the youth justice system and comparison groups of b) children who had been in contact with the youth justice system and who were not looked after and c) looked after children who had not been in contact with the youth justice system;
- interviews with all three samples of young people, including narrative accounts, developmental measures and an analysis of attitudes and decision-making (drawing on social/psychological frameworks);
- interagency focus groups in the four local authorities to explore local practice and protocols for supporting young people in care and offending/at risk of offending.

The study

Research governance and ethical approval
The project had approval from the Association of Directors of Children's Services (ADCS) Research Committee, the support of the Youth Justice Board and ethical approval from the UEA School of Social Work Ethics Committee.

Stakeholder group
Stakeholder engagement was a key strength of this project. The stakeholder group consisted of senior representatives of statutory and voluntary bodies concerned with the welfare of looked after children and children who offend. A series of meetings was held during the project with the stakeholder group to discuss the research process and issues arising for policy and practice.

Young people's reference group
Voice (a national advocacy charity for young people who are or have been in care) set up a young people's reference group specifically for this project. The young people's reference group helped the UEA research team with ideas about recruitment, including designing the recruitment postcard. The group also helped pilot interview materials. Additional piloting of the interviews was conducted with members of a separate "children in care" group who had recent and direct experience of the youth justice system. Discussions also took place with the reference group about some of the findings, especially findings from the interviews with young people.

Book outline
In this book we begin by providing a review of the legal, policy, practice and research literature in relation to looked after children and offending. This is followed by a review of the research on risk and protective factors for offending. This chapter also provides a detailed account of the key developmental processes in areas such as attachment, moral development and empathy. These are significant in both

understanding offending by children in care but also in supporting effective caregiving and planning interventions.

The methodology of the study is followed by chapters that set out three areas: findings from the national survey and focus groups; risk and resilience profiles of young people in the study; and findings from the qualitative interviews with young people.

The book concludes with models of risk and resilience for care and offending pathways, integrating what we know from the wider body of research and from this study, and suggesting implications for policy and practice.

2 Looked after children and offending: legal, policy, practice and research context

Understanding the pathways of looked after children who are at risk of offending or who have committed offences requires an understanding of a range of legal, policy, practice and research contexts – and the ways in which they interact. Government policy in this field, in particular, has to some extent been driven by research evidence, but has often been a driver of research by the funding of research and evaluation programmes. The legal framework dictates certain procedures and practice in relation to care and to offending, but the detail of developments in local areas may be constrained by legal requirements or may work creatively within them.

All of these policy and practice contexts also connect with different and interacting disciplines. Thus we cannot make sense of young people's experiences and pathways without considering both the psychology of child and adolescent development, including, in particular, the impact of abuse and neglect, and the social contexts of, for example, gang culture on the one hand or pro-social peer groups on the other, in which individual young people's identities are being created. Although much of the psychology of development, maltreatment and offending is dealt with in the following chapter on risk and resilience, implicit or explicit sets of assumptions about what children and young people need to thrive developmentally and become pro-social citizens in adulthood are discussed in this chapter, as they underpin child care legislation, policy, practice and research.

We first review the policy context for care and youth justice in the period since the Children Act 1989, then explore the research on outcomes for children in care, considering the place of offending alongside other concerns.

Law, policy and practice for children in state care

The challenge of meeting the needs of children who have suffered adverse parenting, abuse and neglect and become looked after by the local authority has been the focus of significant policy and research activity, particularly in the 20-year period since the implementation of the Children Act 1989. The Children Act 1989 saw a separation between child welfare matters, in private and public law, and youth justice. The separate development of children's social services and youth offending services since has had the potential to cause difficulties and tensions, but there has been a recognition of the need for both services to work together, not only in respect of those children in state care who offend but in relation to *all* children who offend, many of whom are "children in need" (Children Act 1989, s17) or come from "troubled families".

The management of children in care since the Children Act 1989 has been dominated by the Looked after Children (LAC) framework, which uses seven developmental dimensions, i.e. health, education, emotional and behavioural development, identity, family and social relationships, social presentation, and self-care skills, as the basis for assessment, planning and review of all children in care. The LAC system is very detailed and was designed to improve outcomes for children in care by focusing on a developmental and ecological model and by placing certain procedural obligations on all local authorities, e.g. LAC reviews of the child's care plan every six months; detailed documentary evidence of the child's progress on these dimensions; and the required involvement of other key agencies, including health, education and, where relevant, the youth offending service.

However, by 1998, concerns about outcomes for children in care, especially in relation to education and placement stability, and in light of the inquiries into historic abuse in residential care, resulted in *Quality Protects* (Department for Education and Skills – DfES, 1998). This was a landmark government initiative, which continues to resonate in policy and practice today. *Quality Protects* aimed to improve outcomes for children in need and children looked after by the local authority and was accompanied by a funded research initiative.

Quality Protects was distinctive in explicitly emphasising the responsibility for children in care, not just of social services departments, but also of councillors as "corporate parents", challenging them to provide these vulnerable children with care of the high quality that they would wish to see for their own children. Local authorities were required to produce a Management Action Plan (MAP), associated with a wide range of performance targets that were designed to ensure that standards were maintained across the country in relation to key areas such as stability, care planning, education, health and leaving care. Central government paid a specific grant to social services departments for looked after children, which was linked to the MAP and to performance measures, and which required extensive collection of administrative data concerning local authority practice and outcomes for looked after children. A series of further legal and policy developments rapidly followed, in particular, the introduction of the Children (Leaving Care) Act 2000.

The death of Victoria Climbié in 2000 and the subsequent Laming Inquiry shifted the focus of concern towards child protection. However, in the *Every Child Matters* Green Paper in 2003, Lord Laming took the opportunity to set out five universal objectives for all children: being healthy; staying safe; enjoying and achieving; making a positive contribution; and achieving economic well-being. These desired outcomes were reinforced in 2004 by *Every Child Matters: The next steps* and *Every Child Matters: Change for children*, which focused on agencies working together. Although the five *Every Child Matters* outcomes were built into policy at all levels at the time, for looked after children the seven LAC dimensions have continued to be used as a basis for planning and review of children in care (Department for Children Schools and Families – DCSF, 2010a).

The Children Act (2004) implemented a number of the reforms proposed in *Every Child Matters*, in particular, the creation of Children's Services Departments that brought together education and social services for children, the setting up of Local Safeguarding Children's Boards to facilitate interagency working, and the establishment of the Children's Commissioner for England. All of these have had implications not only for services for looked after children, but also for the engagement of agencies, including the youth offending service, in a shared corporate responsibility for looked after children.

A parallel set of developments during the 1990s in adoption policy and practice led via lengthy consultations to the Adoption and Children Act 2002. This was implemented in 2005 and was linked to a programme of research (www.adoptionresearchinitiative.org.uk). Policy development in relation to adoption is highly relevant to the UK's approach to the general population of looked after children, because in reinforcing the commitment to achieving adoption, where appropriate, for children in care, the political debate has sometimes become polarised around emphasising the benefits of adoption by contrasting it with the presumed negative consequences for children who remain long-term in care, including the risk of offending.

Some of the same concerns about looked after children that had led to *Quality Protects* in 1998, in particular, around education and stability, surfaced again in the Green Paper in 2006, *Care Matters: Transforming the lives of children and young people in care*. There followed an extensive consultation process, resulting in the White Paper *Care Matters: Time for change* (DfES, 2007), which under-pinned the Children and Young Persons Act 2008. The areas addressed in the White Paper were corporate parenting; family and parenting support; care placements; education; health and well-being; transition to adulthood; and the role of the practitioner. The foreword to this White Paper by the then Secretary of State for Education and Skills, Alan Johnson, reflects the tone of much of the debate before and since 2007 regarding the care system. He stated: 'We are determined to improve the plight of children in care' (p. 4), although also suggesting that there was some good work with good outcomes for these children.

Care Matters: Time for change (2007) suggested a number of models to promote improved practice. It focused significantly on education and the need to raise standards, for example, through the Personal Education Plan (PEP), for all looked after children. It recognised the special needs of looked after children who come from backgrounds of adversity and highlighted work on resilience as providing an important and positive theoretical framework for working with children in care (Masten, 2001 in DCSF, 2007, p. 19).

Attachment has also been a key framework for promoting children's development and well-being. Schofield and Beek's Secure Base model (Schofield and Beek, 2006, 2014), which draws on both attachment and resilience theories, was recommended for training foster carers and helping children to be more 'confident and competent' (DCSF, 2007, pp. 45–47). This model has since been incorporated into the Fostering Network's *Skills to Foster* training programme for new foster carers.

The emphasis in *Care Matters* on evidence-based practice led to widespread encouragement for and government investment in social learning theory based foster care models, originating in the Oregon Social Learning Center, e.g. Multi-dimensional Treatment Foster Care (MTFC) (Fisher *et al*, 2009). MTFC is particularly relevant for young people in care and at risk of offending as it was first developed as an alternative to custody for young offenders and is a highly structured placement intervention with the aim of changing anti-social behaviour. Research by Biehal *et al* (2012) has explored the use of MTFC in the care context in England.

For residential care, the key initiative arising from *Care Matters* was the piloting of social pedagogy, introduced from Germany and Scandinavia where social pedagogues are trained at degree level. Not unlike certain existing therapeutic approaches to residential care in the UK, social pedagogy combines an education-focused response, including introducing young people to activities, with a focus on building nurturing relationships between staff and young people (Berridge *et al*, 2011a, b).

In relation to leaving care, there was the introduction of both the *Right2BCared4* pathfinders (to promote children in care staying to age 18) and the *Staying Put* pilot projects (to promote the option for young people of staying in their foster family up to the age of 21).[1] These initiatives are highly relevant for young people who may be at particular risk of offending in the teenage years and at the point of

---

1   It is now government policy for young people to be given the option of staying in foster care up to the age of 21.

leaving care, but as subsequent chapters providing data from the survey and from young people's own stories show, these require not only policy commitment but also flexible resources that local authorities may not have or may not make available.

An emphasis on the scrutiny of *care plans* for looked after children and the need to monitor children's well-being and local authorities as corporate parents through the work of the Independent Reviewing Officers (IROs, first introduced in 2004) became seen as a key part of the *Care Matters* strategy to improve outcomes. The IRO role was also seen as a way of reassuring the courts that court-approved care plans would be followed through. In 2010, new guidance and regulations were issued for *Care Planning, Placement and Case Review* (DCSF, 2010a) and an accompanying *IRO Handbook* was published (DCSF, 2010b). These jointly strengthened the role of the LAC review process and that of the IRO, while reinforcing some of the key principles that had been developed following the Children Act 1989 – in particular, a commitment to achieving permanence and an acceptance of a range of legitimate permanence options that included the birth family, kinship care, long-term foster care, special guardianship and adoption.

These guidance documents were intended to shape the management of care pathways through to adulthood, so it was important that children who are both in care and within the youth justice system were recognised as a special case in the guidance. The IRO's responsibilities are therefore said to include:

> *Making sure that the child's care plan addresses any unmet needs that may lead to offending and that, if appropriate, targeted services designed to prevent offending are provided. It is also important to consider the suitability of the placement in managing behavioural problems.* (DCSF, 2010b, p. 34)

Although the first responsibility for ensuring well-being and good outcomes for looked after children, including pro-social behaviour, rests with the corporate parent, the responsible social worker and other agencies involved in providing services to looked after children, the LAC review process and the IRO are expected to play a significant role in monitoring and promoting the well-being and outcomes for looked after children, including in relation to offending. The Family Justice Review Panel (2011) recommended that, with a reduction in the time cases take in court to an average of 26 weeks, the responsibility for the detail of care planning will pass from the courts to the local authority, with the IRO role receiving a further boost in expectations regarding the development and monitoring of plans.

Also included in the *Care Planning, Placement and Case Review* (DCSF, 2010a) was a new "sufficiency" duty that has an impact on managing placement choice for children and young people at risk of offending. Each local authority providing children's services must now take steps to secure, 'so far as reasonably practicable', sufficient accommodation within its area to meet the needs of children whom it is looking after – but also in some cases for children in need who are at risk of care or custody. However, it is also stated that children should not be moved from out of authority placements for the sole purpose of meeting the sufficiency duty if their needs are being met by the existing range of services. Placement choice for high-risk young people and the subsequent provision of other services for those placed outside of the authority – or indeed those placed into the area by other authorities – raise many challenges for both looked after children services and youth offending services. The emphasis on keeping young people closer to their home area will hopefully stimulate greater efforts to provide or commission appropriate foster and residential accommodation that will allow young people to maintain important relationships and feel less isolated. However, the flexible focus on the needs of each young person is also very necessary, as for some young people the availability of specialist provision or the active benefits of distance from anti-social peer groups will be factors that need to be taken into account.

The most recent relevant initiative affecting children's services, and therefore the provision of services to looked after children, has been the *Munro Review of Child Protection* (DfE, 2011a) following the death of Peter Connolly. The focus of this review report was on the nature of social work as a professional activity and the organisational systems that surround it. The criticisms of a perceived over-bureaucratic child protection system have led to recommendations for much more local and individual judgements to be made about, for example, assessment processes. The LAC system has provided a bureaucratic framework that allows for some consistency of practice at a challenging time, with increased numbers of looked after children, but there is also an expectation that professional judgement will be exercised by social workers, IROs and others in relation to managing the review process in a child-centred way.

As Blades *et al* (2011) have pointed out, there has been no proposed structure for tackling offending by looked after children, such as the virtual school heads appointed to improve educational outcomes. However, at national and local levels there have been attempts to reduce, in particular, the unnecessary criminalisation of looked after children, with a number of initiatives, such as the requirement for protocols between police and residential homes in relation to avoiding inappropriate arrest and charging of young people. This and other approaches are explored further in later chapters based on data from this study.

Policy in youth justice

One of the dominant debates historically in the development of youth justice policy, and which explains something of the difficulty in addressing the question of looked after children and offending, has been between justice and welfare approaches. However, the fact that the debate has been long-running does not mean that there have been easy solutions. As Muncie and Hughes (2002) put it:

> The history of youth justice is a history of conflict, contradictions, ambiguity and compromise. Conflict is inevitable in a system that has traditionally pursued the twin goals of welfare and justice . . . As a result it continually seeks the compromise between youth as a special deserving case and youth as fully responsible for their own actions. (cited in Dugmore *et al*, 2006, p. 29)

The separation of children's welfare matters from youth justice in the Children Act 1989 has meant that the youth justice service has needed to conduct its own balancing act in relation to justice and welfare. In 1998, the same year as *Quality Protects*, the Youth Justice Board (YJB) was established, and led to the development of multi-agency youth offending services, which linked children's social care, education, health, probation and the police.

At local level the youth offending teams developed a range of programmes that addressed prevention as well as intervention, hence the Youth Intervention Programmes (YIPs) for 13- to 16-year-olds and the Youth Inclusion Support Panel (YISP) teams, which sought to prevent social exclusion, offending and anti-social behaviour by offering support services, primarily to high-risk eight- to 13-year-olds. At this level, welfare concerns are paramount, with the aim of building in individual and environmental protective factors to prevent children coming into the criminal justice system.

Policy concerns for all young people in custody, including those looked after, have not been only about their welfare while in custody, but also about re-offending rates, which are damaging to young people and to society. This has led to a range of alternatives, not only diversionary strategies and alternative sentences that include a strong welfare element, such as the referral order, but also entirely new approaches, such as the development of *restorative justice*.

The practice of restorative justice as a method for dealing with offending has a history that goes back to the 1970s, when it was developed in New Zealand, Australia, Canada and the USA. It has its origins in practices associated with indigenous communities where offences against individuals were conceptualised as offences against the community, and a community approach, which included elements of reparation, was therefore often taken to resolve the situation. The principles and practice of victim–offender mediation and community mediation emerged in Britain in the 1980s and are now not only well-established here but across the world, with the United Nations (2002) endorsing restorative justice as a constructive and valued way for a society to deal with offending, especially in relation to youth justice.

There are now advocates in the UK for the use of restorative justice in relation to children's behaviour in the wider community, e.g. in schools, as well as through police responses to offending, e.g. community or neighbourhood resolutions.

The original victim–offender restorative justice conference was intended to provide the victim with the opportunity to tell their story and obtain recognition for their feelings, and to provide the offender with the opportunity to tell their story, to express their feelings and remorse. Reparation may be to the victim or the community. Both the victim and the offender need to be well prepared for the conference and it requires some capacity in the offender to reflect on their own feelings and the feelings of others. As will be discussed in the following chapter and as emerges from the study, the offender's capacity to engage in this process may well be affected by experiences of childhood maltreatment, characteristic of children in care, that lead to difficulties with social cognition and empathy.

Consideration of the growing role of restorative justice is very relevant for this study, not only because of its use in the youth justice system, but also because it now often underpins the handling of challenging behaviour in residential care. Restorative justice in residential care is intended to play a role in both reducing anti-social behaviour through a process of emotional and moral education, but also reducing criminalisation of children by reducing the need to involve the police and the court.

As adult prison numbers continued to grow and as re-offending rates remained high, the Ministry of Justice presented a Green Paper for consultation titled *Breaking the Cycle* (Ministry of Justice, 2010a). This linked youth and adult offending in one of its overall aims:

> To break the cycle of crime and prison which creates new victims every day. Despite a 50 per cent increase in the budget for prisons and managing offenders in the last ten years, almost half of all adult offenders released from custody reoffend within a year. It is also not acceptable that 75 per cent of offenders sentenced to youth custody reoffend within a year. If we do not prevent and tackle offending by young people then the young offenders of today will become the prolific career criminals of tomorrow.

Specific goals for youth justice were therefore set out:

To prevent young people committing crime and beginning a pattern of criminal behaviour that could last into adulthood, we will:

- *encourage Youth Offending Teams to improve the quality of work with parents including through greater use of parenting orders where parents will not face up to their responsibilities;*
- *simplify out-of-court disposals; and*
- *increase the use of restorative justice.*

The emphasis on parents taking responsibility for young people's behaviour has challenging implications where the child is in care, the parent is a corporate parent, and "parenting" is provided by foster carers and residential workers.

It is important to note that, unlike the adult prison population, the overall numbers of young people under 18 imprisoned in England and Wales fell by a third in 2008–11, from 3,000 to 2,000 (Allen, 2011), which is an encouraging development. But as Berelowitz and Hibbert (2011) pointed out, England continues to lock up more children aged 10 to 17 than any other European country.

Research context

In the period since the Children Act 1989, there has been significant investment by a range of funders, but in particular the Government, in research into pathways and outcomes for looked after children, with each of the policy initiatives listed above generating new research and evaluation studies. The field has also been able to benefit from some useful administrative data, collected annually from local authorities, which here is woven into the research evidence on the characteristics of children in care and in the youth justice system. The focus here is on a summary of some of the key research specifically relevant for this study and the links between care and offending.

Characteristics of looked after children

There were 65,520 children looked after on 31 March 2011 (DfE, 2011), with 56 per cent boys and 44 per cent girls. The majority were aged 10+ (58%) and in foster care (74%), with nine per cent living in residential children's homes.

For this cohort of children, 62 per cent had a "need code" when they were first looked after of abuse and neglect. However, other research on children who are in long-term foster care having come into care in early or middle childhood found that there is abuse and/ or neglect in the history of almost all – 90 per cent (Schofield *et al*, 2010) – thereby suggesting that children who remain in care are very likely to have experienced some form of maltreatment prior to care.

The majority of children who remain in care come from family backgrounds of parental difficulty, with the Schofield *et al* study (2011, 2012) of 230 children with long-term foster care plans finding that 59 per cent of mothers had mental health problems, 33 per cent misused alcohol and 32 per cent misused drugs. Such figures suggest not only that parenting quality was likely to have been compromised when children were cared for at home, but also that ongoing contact needs to be carefully managed.

Care planning and permanence

Since the 1980s, the goal of care planning and indeed care in the UK has been closely associated with the concept of permanence (Maluccio *et al*, 1986; Thoburn *et al*, 1986; Sinclair *et al*, 2007; Biehal *et al*, 2010; Schofield *et al*, 2010, 2011). The significance of permanence in a family where the child can grow up through to adulthood is that it provides not only stability and continuity, but also a sense of belonging and family membership. Permanence options can include leaving care through return home, placement with extended family members, long-term foster care, special guardianship or adoption (DCSF, 2010a). For children who remain in care, their permanence option will be a foster family, with the birth family likely to remain part of the picture (Schofield *et al*, 2010; Schofield and Ward, 2011). However, the permanence plan for children who come into care aged 14 to 16 is more difficult to establish when there is a current risk of maltreatment or anti-social behaviour in the birth family and substitute families are neither straightforward to identify nor necessarily what the young people say they want.

In research on permanence there have been studies to identify the benefits and risks of each permanence option and to track cohorts of children. Sinclair's major study of the care system (Sinclair *et al*, 2007) provided a valuable analysis of the patterns and pathways of children in care. Particularly relevant for the current study were the differences they identified between "adolescent graduates", who had come into care under the age of 11, primarily from backgrounds of neglect and abuse, and "adolescent entrants", a small number of whom came into care for reasons of abuse and neglect, but the majority of whom came into care following difficulties with their behaviour at school and with their families. While acknowledging the significance of the goal of permanence, Sinclair *et al* (2007) found that only 20 per cent of adolescent graduates had achieved a placement lasting five years or more and, for adolescent entrants, lengthy placements were even less likely in the time available. However, they concluded that, although the goal of permanence was hard to achieve, reliable and nurturing relationships in a child's life are of paramount importance, whether those relationships are in foster care, residential care, kinship care or adoption. So finding and supporting such relationships must continue to be the focus of professional efforts.

Although this research raised concerns about stability in care, an important piece of research led by Biehal *et al* (2010) compared long-term foster care with adoption and found that emotional and behavioural outcomes for children in *stable* foster placements were similar to adoption. This is an important contribution to our understanding of the potential of long-term foster care to provide both a sense of belonging and good outcomes, although the emphasis on the significance of stability is also clear.

Schofield and Beek's work on foster care (Beek and Schofield, 2004; Schofield and Beek, 2006, 2009; Schofield *et al*, 2011) has focused on planned long-term foster care and drawn together the benefits of sensitive parenting in the Secure Base model, based on attachment, with the key principles of permanence around family membership and belonging.

The interacting dimensions of availability that develops trust, sensitivity that helps the child to manage their feelings, acceptance that builds self-esteem, and co-operation that helps children feel effective come from attachment theory and research (Ainsworth *et al*, 1971) and research on foster care (Beek and Schofield, 2004). The addition of the dimension of family membership to the model has been shown to be helpful in explaining what builds security and resilience in older fostered children, including adolescents – and is equally relevant for children adopted from care (Schofield and Beek, 2006). Secure Base caregiving, where these dimensions are present, reduces the child's anxiety and enables the child to explore, learn and fulfil their potential. For children from backgrounds of abuse and neglect, this can have a therapeutic effect in helping to overcome developmental delay and difficulties. Security in attachment relationships is linked to a range of protective factors, such as acceptance or empathy, that reduce the likelihood of anti-social behaviour and offending and promote resilience – as discussed in the following chapter.

One of the key elements in any model of permanence or in thinking about the outcomes for looked after children is the challenge of leaving care (Stein, 2009, 2012). In spite of the research and policy initiatives in this area of practice, which have kept the issue high on the agenda for the care system, the transition to adulthood presents particular issues for young people leaving care and at risk of offending. Given the concerns about vulnerabilities and criminal pathways in adult life, research continues to reinforce our concerns about this critical period for looked after children, who often lack a supportive and pro-social family base (Stein, 2012).

Residential care

Although sensitive care and therapeutic relationships are also possible in residential care, government policy and local authority practice on placement choice for looked after children have increasingly been in favour of foster care (74% of looked after children in foster care, DfE,

2011) rather than residential care. Berridge *et al* (2011b, p. 5) describe 'a steady decline in the use of residential care from 32 per cent of the care population in 1978, to 21 per cent in 1986, to only nine per cent in 2010/11'.

This decline in the use of residential care has led to it becoming increasingly a placement for older and more difficult children, who are not able to be cared for in foster care or who do not wish to be fostered. Some teenage children may come straight into residential care when they become looked after, but others may have been through a succession of short-term foster homes or experienced deterioration of their behaviour in adolescence or the breakdown of a long-term placement in foster care or adoption.

In Berridge *et al*'s study of residential care (Berridge *et al*, 2011b), they found that it was difficult to make direct connections between quality of care and outcomes, although they were able to observe a range of care, including very sensitive care, and young people were appreciative of the setting and good relationships with staff, when they occurred. Peer relationships in residential care and peer conflict, however, remain a problem for young people (Barter, 2007). Other work indicates that the care environment in residential homes may contribute to the likelihood of a young person offending, if less consistent care increases the influence of already delinquent peers (Taylor, 2006).

Berridge *et al* (2011b, p. 98) conclude that certain key factors could help to make residential care more effective and provide higher levels of care, i.e. homes being smaller, not taking short-term emergencies and having better qualified heads of homes. Where children's homes are to provide a home for young people during crucial periods of their adolescence, the need to minimise movement in and out of the home and achieve a settled group is likely to be key to stabilising young people and giving them a secure base.

A recent study by Hayden (2010) specifically of residential care and offending over a seven-year period asked the question: 'Is children's residential care a "criminogenic" environment?' and concluded:

The residential care environment, particularly for older teen-

agers, often presents a set of risks that tend to reinforce offending behaviour and this is in part due to its "last resort" status. (Hayden, 2010, p. 1)

The risks in residential care identified by Hayden included risks in the individual young person; risks of peer dynamics that reinforce offending; risks where young people are out of education; and systemic risks of criminalisation where protocols with the police are not carefully observed.

These risks can all be managed and mitigated to some degree, but it is unlikely that the last resort status of residential care will entirely change. So, the research suggests, it is necessary to attempt to differentiate children according to age, stage and plan within residential care in order to treat each placement positively, especially where additional support may turn a young person away from negative pathways.

Given the *parallel concerns about education and offending outcomes* for looked after children, it is helpful to consider the research on education outcomes for children in care alongside research on offending. The main areas of overlap are in relation to two key points. The first is that risk factors that predict care, such as low economic status and abuse and neglect, also predict poor educational achievement (Berridge, 2007) and offending (Loeber and Farrington, 2000; Darker *et al*, 2008). Secondly, age at entry to care affects key measures of educational outcomes (i.e. GCSE results) and offending (i.e. some young people are already offending before they enter care in the teenage years). Therefore, understanding the impact of age and stage is crucial to drawing conclusions on which policy might be built in both areas. As Berridge points out, for example, 50 per cent of looked after children who take GCSEs came into care after the age of 14, which, in addition to the risk factors in children's background, would suggest very good reasons why care is not able to reverse significant prior educational underachievement, and certainly challenges the suggestion that care "causes" poor GCSE results. However, the fact that looked after children are at higher risk in relation to both education and offending means that the care system needs to target resources for the adolescents based on an understanding of those risks in order to mitigate their impact.

In relation to offending pathways, it is clear from the study by Darker *et al* (2008) of 250 children in care aged 10 to 17 that there is a complex picture of children moving into and out of care and offending in the teenage years and there are no simple causal explanations. They concluded that, although the majority of young people in care were not offenders, the care system needs to be more effective at dealing with established offending behaviour, but prevention is key:

> *Whilst a greater number of the young people had committed offences than in the general population, the vast majority were law abiding. For those who did offend, the care episode itself was unlikely to have been the sole cause of their delinquency. The findings suggest that the services offered once the young people entered local authority care did not succeed in combating established offending behaviour. Perhaps initiatives targeted in the community prior to entry to care may be more effective.* (Darker *et al*, 2008, p. 1)

The research on youth offending indicates that it is the existence of multiple risk factors that makes a young person most vulnerable to offending and that these cumulative and interactive risks exist across family, community and individual levels (e.g. Darker *et al*, 2008). What is also important for the overlap between offending and the care population are the significant transition points in a young person's life, such as moving from school to work, from family to care or from care to independent living, which can trigger or exacerbate offending. These transition points can, however, also be points of opportunity to find personal strengths or identify new external resources and reverse downward spirals (Rutter, 2006).

One increasingly important area of research for practice has been in relation to the connections between mental health problems and youth offending and between mental health problems and poor outcomes from care – and so a possible common causation of problems in care and in offending. The Office of the Children's

Commissioner conducted a study titled '*I think I must have been born bad*' – *emotional well-being and mental health of children and young people in the youth justice system* (Berelowitz and Hibbert, 2011), which focused on both mental health and learning difficulties among young people in custody. The study's recommendations included the importance of identifying young people's mental health and other needs alongside recognition of their rights to appropriate care and advocacy.

Our understanding of the complex relationship between care and offending (Taylor, 2006) can benefit from an understanding of how that relationship is experienced by young people themselves, as reflected in the qualitative research by a team at the National Children's Bureau (Blades *et al*, 2011). This study reported on inter-views with 23 children in care aged 13 to 17. The majority of these young people were either in custody or had previously been in custody, although some had no formal involvement with the youth justice system. Their findings showed a complex picture, with a range of pathways as children talked about their involvement with both the care system and the youth justice system. Young people highlighted a number of risk factors in the care system in relation to offending, i.e. loss of, or infrequent contact with, family and friends; poor relation-ships with carers and social workers; difficult relationships with peers/ peer pressure; type and number of placements. About the youth justice system there was less clarity about what helped in relation to preventing re-offending by looked after children, but the young people highlighted the quality of relationships with the professionals as the most important factor.

Summary

- Almost all children in care are from backgrounds of deprivation, poor parenting, abuse and neglect – factors that together are risk factors for a range of emotional, social and behavioural difficulties, including anti-social and offending behaviour.
- The care system has the goal of achieving permanence, providing a

family in which children can grow safely and securely to adulthood. Permanence options include reunification with the birth family, kinship care, long-term foster care, special guardianship and adoption.

- Research suggests that all of these options can meet children's physical, emotional, health, educational and family membership needs. However, the age at which children enter care, the genetic risk, the history of abuse and neglect and the degree of emotional and behavioural difficulties will affect the stability and outcomes of placements. So also will systemic factors, such as delays in the placement and court system, the availability of high quality family and residential placements, and the support available from education, health and youth offending services.

- Adolescence and leaving care are times of both opportunity and high risk, especially for those who have mental health problems or who are offenders. Although leaving care has been the focus of research-based legislation and guidance and there is some excellent practice, it remains a period in which resources are stretched and young people can slip through the net.

- Youth offending services have developed constructive models for prevention and intervention, in particular, in relation to restorative justice. They are required to work in partnership with children's services to reduce offending by looked after children.

- Protocols between the police and residential care are widely used to address the problem of the inappropriate criminalisation of looked after children through court appearances regarding minor offences in their placements. However, concerns remain as to how well protocols and other strategies have been implemented in some areas.

- Although the position is complex, all young people in care and at risk of offending highlight the significance of a reliable relationship with a caring adult.

3 Research on risk and resilience factors for offending

Reducing the crime rate is always of importance to communities and government for both personal safety and economic reasons. Criminal activity by young people is a particular concern, as an early criminal record adds a significant barrier to future employment opportunity and has a strong association with future re-offending. A risk-based approach to studying offending is well established (Loeber and Farrington, 1999) and has been useful to policy-makers and practitioners because specific factors have been identified that have strong links to offending. Identifying specific factors and pathways for offending can help in the prioritisation of resources targeted at reducing offending. For young offenders, there is a particular interest in the role that child development plays in the activation of delinquent behaviour. Risk-based approaches have also been used to examine other negative outcomes for children in care, such as poor educational achievement or poor mental health (Berridge, 2007; Guglani et al, 2008). Negative outcomes, such as youth offending, poor educational achievement or poor mental health, often arise from similar risks. Therefore, interventions to mitigate these common risks are particularly cost effective because they seek to prevent multiple negative outcomes.

Vulnerable groups of young people can be identified through risk-based screening and targeted for preventative interventions. This is particularly the case for young people in care who have been exposed to severe levels of harm, often at a very young age (e.g. Franzen et al, 2008). The advantage of examining risk over the life course is that the impact of types of risk and the timing of risk exposure can also be examined. This knowledge is particularly helpful for planning interventions, as individuals can be targeted for risk type, and they can also be targeted for interventions during certain 'windows of opportunity' during development for optimum impact (Masten, 2004).

Running in parallel to risk-based study, resilience scholars have examined factors that appear to protect children and young people from succumbing to the negative effects of adverse experience. Key authors in this field include Michael Rutter, who studied high-risk children who, in spite of experiencing adverse circumstances, adjusted well to adult life (Rutter, 1987). Another important researcher in resilience is Ann Masten, whose work with children of schizophrenic mothers focused on the adaptive processes children use to adjust to adversity (Masten *et al*, 1990). The advantage of considering resilience in addition to risk is that the concept of resilience introduces a *wellness* theoretical model compared to a *deficit* model. It is helpful to consider both approaches, as risk and resilience are not always dimensional; the opposite of risk is not always resilience. In addition, the processes promoting resilience are different from the processes that increase risk. These two theoretical perspectives can provide practitioners and policy-makers with a two-pronged approach to reducing negative outcomes by both mitigating the impact of risk factors and encouraging the presence of protective factors.

The research examining risk factors associated with offending and protective factors against offending considers these factors in probabilistic terms, i.e. the likelihood of offending given exposure to certain risk or protective factors. Risk and protective factors are evaluated using the strength of their correlation with offending behaviours. Using a risk-based approach means it is possible to get an idea about the *relative contributions* of risk factors, but it is not possible to infer from these associations the *direct causes* of offending. Nonetheless, in considering the evidence on risk and protective factors and offending as a whole, it is possible to indicate which risk and protective factors are related to offending as this helps to give some direction for prioritising further research and interventions.

While this chapter provides an overview of risk and resilience for the outcome of offending for all young people, the pertinent risk and resilience factors for young people *in care* are highlighted. In this chapter we outline some established theoretical perspectives on youth offending which use the risk and resilience paradigm. We examine the concepts of risk and resilience within a developmental framework and take a bio-psychosocial perspective incorporating biological, psychological and social context factors relevant during particular phases of development. The chapter ends with a summary of known risk and resilience factors for offending.

Conceptualising risk

There are a number of theoretical frameworks conceptualising risk and resilience, which provide a useful starting point when considering risks for offending for young people and these are outlined in turn. This outline is then followed by an examination of the research evidence to date about the types of risk and resilience factors known to be associated with offending.

It is also important to consider risk and resilience for offending for young people within a developmental context, so we summarise the normal developmental pathway for social and moral development, both in early childhood and adolescence, and examine the impact of negative experiences on this pathway. A successful transition to adulthood depends largely on the ability to navigate complex social worlds; therefore we also examine the role of social cognition development in relation to offending.

Risk typology

A well-known theoretical framework for youth offending is Moffitt's developmental taxonomy (Moffitt, 1993). Moffitt's longitudinal work defined two types of young offender: the life course persistent offender and the adolescent limited offender. The life course persistent offender is a young person characterised by the early onset of anti-social behaviour that continues throughout the life span and who is influenced by *distal* risk factors (often beyond the control of the young person), such as foetal exposure to alcohol and inherited neuropsychological deficits. Moffitt argues that it is the interaction of these innate deficits with poor environments, such as poverty and poor parenting, that exposes these individuals to greater levels of risk.

In contrast, the adolescent limited offender is characterised by the late onset of anti-social behaviour that is limited to the adolescent years and seen to be influenced by *proximal* (immediately surrounding the young person) risk factors, such as peer influence. Moffitt suggests that adolescent limited offenders experience "normal" parenting and childhood, but experience a "maturity gap" in adolescence whereby they seek to gain the identity of adulthood, such as independence and autonomy. Associating with life course persistent offenders at this age can highlight to adolescents the maturity gap, as life course persistent offenders demonstrate independence and autonomy through the use of drink and drugs, illegal driving and acquisition of consumer goods. Moffitt (1993) has argued through use of criminal conviction statistics that the majority of young offenders fall into the adolescent limited offending group and that it is only a small proportion of young offenders who can be classified as life course persistent offenders.

Empirical evidence indicates that predictors for adolescent limited offenders include associating with anti-social peers, having a personality trait of social potency (vulnerable to social influence) and usually committing non-violent offences. Predictors of life course persistent offenders are: early onset of anti-social behaviour; committing many offences over a long period of time; personality traits of impulsivity; attention deficit/hyperactivity symptoms; neuropsychological deficits; and difficult temperaments (Moffitt and Caspi, 2001).

The implications for practice of Moffitt's theory are that if most youth desist from offending over time then custody should be avoided for these young people. This is because custody is more likely to encourage the continuation of criminal behaviour through increased exposure to life course persistent offenders and through creating barriers to integration back into employment or education on release. One implication of categorising some young offenders as life course persistent offenders is that custody should be reserved for these offenders. However, this assumes that it is possible to identify discrete categories of young offenders as Moffitt describes. Skardhamar (2009), in a critique of Moffitt's taxonomy, highlights issues with the empirical evidence that Moffitt (2006) provides to support her theory and also raises theoretical anomalies. He suggests that creating a categorical typology precludes the examination of a *dimensional* approach to youth offenders so that, at one end of the dimension, we would see high exposure to early innate and environmental risk factors compared to minimal exposure to innate and environmental risk factors at the other end of the dimension. Skardhamar (2009) suggests that this approach would better account for the empirical evidence which shows different numbers of groups, different aetiologies and differing ages of onset of offending.

A further caveat to the age emphasis that Moffitt's model implies is evidenced by a longitudinal study by Elliott *et al* (1989), which indicates that age at onset is not a strong enough predictor on its own. They found from the US National Youth Survey that violent behaviour observed before the age of 11 years was associated with a 50 per cent chance of persistence to adulthood, but reduced to 30 per cent if observed between the age of 11 and 13 years and even further to 10 per cent post 13 years. They show that there is a decline in likelihood of continuation of offending with age of onset, and that even with early onset offending, the likelihood is still only a 50:50 ratio (Elliott *et al*, 1989).

Risk-based models

In contrast to a typology approach to offending, risk-based models take a *cumulative deficit* view of offending whereby each individual can be assessed in terms of their exposure to known predictors of offending, working on the assumption that those individuals with a high number of risk factors should be targeted for interventions to mitigate these risks (Pungello *et al*, 1996; Sameroff *et al*, 1998; Ackerman *et al*, 1999). In addition to the impact of the number of risk factors that individuals are exposed to during their development, timing of their exposure is also critical. This is the case, both in terms of the overwhelming nature of experiencing several risk factors at one time, for example, experiencing abuse from one parent at the same time as losing other support, but also in terms of being exposed to risks at a young age when an individual is less developmentally prepared to be able to cope with the risk, for example, having to care for a parent as a child. What is less clear with the risk approach, however, is whether some risks are more influential than others. Meta-analytic studies examined later in this chapter help give some insight into which risk factors seem to be more influential than others.

Some researchers have examined whether there is a *threshold effect* of risk, beyond which offending becomes more likely. Appleyard *et al* (2005) comment on studies that found a threshold effect whereby negative outcomes increased dramatically after exposure to 3–4 risks, suggesting a trigger point at exposure to 4+ risk factors. However, they also noted that other studies have found a linear effect, whereby negative outcomes increase at the same rate as exposure to risk. Appleyard *et al*'s study, using a longitudinal study of at-risk urban children, tested for both linear and quadratic effects. Results from the study showed significant linear effects of risk, i.e. a steady increase in negative outcome in line with the increase in risk, but no quadratic effects, i.e. no threshold effect whereby negative outcomes occurred after a trigger number of risks. Even though there is still some debate about threshold vs. linear effects, there is general agreement that exposure to more risk factors is associated with an increase in negative outcomes. Consequently, many youth offending prevention and intervention programmes use a multiple risk-based approach to assess individuals entering the youth justice system, including those from care, to inform their management of that young person.

In risk research there have been attempts to see if specific risks predict specific outcomes. For example, experiencing abuse and neglect in childhood is known to be associated with negative outcomes such as poor educational attainment (Berridge, 2007). Such links make it unsurprising that children in care often underperform. However, there has not been much success in linking specific risks to specific outcomes (Dodge and Petit, 2003), primarily because of the complex interweave of possible risk factors for each individual that starts at conception and also because *biological* characteristics then react with many different *environmental* factors. There is also an issue of time-relevant risk factors that are more risky at specific times, but less so at others. There has been more success in identifying specific risk factors with a number of different negative outcomes. Steinberg and Avenevoli (2000) examined the development of psychopathology and found differing clusters of risk associated with the onset of psychopathology during child development compared to clusters of risks associated with the *maintenance* of psychopathology. Individuals also have differential exposure to stressors. Compas *et al* (1993) suggest that some stressors are normative, in that all individuals would be expected to encounter some of them during their development, for example, moving school, taking an exam, managing changing friend-ships. Other stressors, however, are less commonly experienced as a child and can occur in an acute, short and intense experience, such as the sudden death of a parent, or in a chronic manner where the stressor is experienced as an ongoing concern, such as living with the mental illness of a parent.

Risk factors have been conceptualised in terms of two types of risk: static risk factors and dynamic risk factors (Wong *et al*, 2009). Static types of risk factor are things that cannot be changed once they have happened, e.g. being the child of a teenage parent. Identifying static risk factors is useful for predicting future behaviour, but less so for designing treatment interventions for individuals to effect change. Static risk factors are generally most useful for policy and service provider interventions for prevention work. Dynamic risk factors are those that influence current functioning, such as an individual's association with anti-social peers, taking drugs or experiencing emotional trauma. Dynamic risk factors are amenable to change and are particularly important for considering interventions. Both sets of factors are useful for predicting offending, as explored later in this chapter.

Risk, resilience and child development

The degree of influence that risk and protective factors will have on a young person's propensity to offend will vary according to the age of the child and their stage in development. Exposure to risk at a very early age has been established to be associated with many later negative outcomes (e.g. low education attainment, Hinshaw, 1992), primarily because of potential damage to the developing neurological system. This is a particular issue between the ages of nought to three years when the brain is particularly sensitive to environmental influences that will change its structure or function, for example, for developing the essential social abilities of language, face processing and cognition (Patterson *et al*, 2006).

Early childhood

Exposure to chronic risks, such as child maltreatment in the form of physical, sexual or emotional abuse at an early age, have been found to influence children's brain development to the extent that the region of the brain that responds to threat in the environment becomes overdeveloped. At the same time the lack of support, sensitivity and availability of a caregiver, in the context of dealing with a frightening situation, means that areas of the brain associated with the abilities of abstract thought and cognition and thinking about emotion, vital for learning and emotion regulation, become less developed (Perry, 2001). The continued exposure to threat in early childhood has behavioural consequences such as: hypervigilance, a focus on threat-related cues (typically non-verbal), and anxiety and impulsivity. All of these behaviours are adaptive during a threatening event, but become maladaptive when the immediate threat has passed. The importance for infant brain development of having sensitive caregivers in order to develop a secure attachment for infants is outlined by Schore (2001), who reviews the affective neuroscience literature. In sensitive caregiving, the caregiver helps the infant to regulate their maturing limbic system, the brain areas specialised for adapting to a rapidly changing environment. By providing emotion regulation strategies, the attachment relationship facilitates the expansion of the child's coping capacities (Schore, 2001).

Adolescence

While early childhood is an important time for brain development, the brain is still continuing to develop and change during adolescence.

This is particularly the case in the pre-frontal cortex, the part of the brain that controls executive functions such as planning, reasoning, controlling impulses and understanding consequences of behaviour. This brain development occurs at a time of greater independence for the young person during which more decisions have to be made that influence their future lives, but at a time when their brain is not fully developed to enable optimum decisions (Casey *et al*, 2008). Therefore, support during adolescence is important and can also positively help influence brain development. Adolescence is an important developmental period as it is a time of transition from childhood to adulthood and, as Coleman and Hagell (2007) suggest, this transition poses challenges for a young person.

In adolescence, the future is unknown, so young people are anticipating what lies ahead, which brings with it a degree of anxiety. At the same time, a young person is likely to feel a sense of regret in leaving behind childhood and also to feel ambiguous about their status and identity during the transition. It is a major psychological task for young people to take on the responsibilities that come with adult freedoms and to lose the relative safety of childhood status. Masten (2004) emphasised that there are two key turning points during adolescence: from 12 to 14 years and later from 17 to 18 years. In her review of longitudinal evidence, she notes that interventions that take place at 12 years have an immediate effect (12 months after), but that these effects appear to "disappear" during mid-adolescence (14 to 16 years) then reappear from 16 years onwards. The important message from this research appears to be that interventions early in adolescence may have delayed effects and this should be taken into account when evaluating outcomes of interventions.

When we consider the psychological transitions that adolescents need to make as they enter adulthood, we also need to consider the challenges that the social context provides during this transition. In the economic climate of the early 21st century, uncertainty about jobs, education and training for young people adds to feelings of uncertainty about the future. During December–February 2010, 13 per cent (929,000) of young people aged 16 to 24 were unemployed, a rise of 220,000 compared to 2007. Young people make up a larger proportion (38%) of the 2.5 million people of working age who are unemployed (Potton, 2010). For any young person, transition from adolescence to adulthood constitutes a major challenge that requires support to overcome. For those young people who have experienced disadvantage, this transition can be even more daunting and therefore more support will be required. Young people leaving care are a particularly vulnerable group as they are more likely to be living independently at a younger age and they often do not have the family or social support networks that other young people have (Stein, 2006, 2012). For young offenders, having a criminal record and often few educational qualifications, as a result of high levels of truancy and exclusion (Youth Justice Board, 2008), provides an additional barrier to gaining employment or training.

Moral development

An important part of a child's development, particularly in relation to offending, is that of moral reasoning. It is recognised that young children do not have well-developed moral reasoning and debates continue regarding at what age a child can be held accountable for anti-social behaviour. Currently this stands at 10 years in the UK. Cognitive theories of moral development (Piaget, 1932; Kohlberg, 1981) indicate stages of progress in moral thinking, suggesting that around 10 to 11 years, children move from a consequential judgement of an event, e.g. 'How many cups did John break?' to judgements involving intent, e.g. 'Did John intend to break the cup or was it an accident?' In addition, younger children tend to use inflexible rules about what are deemed the "appropriate" actions to take and are less likely to take context into account.

Some theorists position moral concerns as being two distinct domains: behaviours that affect the well-being of others and behaviours that break social rules or norms (Turiel, 1983). Young children are initially more attuned to concerns about the well-being of others and have to learn about social transgressions (Nucci and Weber, 1995). Young children learn to identify the severity of moral and social transgressions from exploration of their environment as they gain feedback from caregivers. For example, children of around two years tend to start to show aggression towards others and objects. Gill and Calkins (2003) found that at this age there is a positive correlation between physical aggression and pro-social behaviour, but that this becomes a negative correlation at later stages of development. Dahl *et al* (2011) suggest that this early stage serves to inform the child of the limits and boundaries to moral transgressions, and that some show of anger at this age is useful for this purpose. They further argue that caregivers provide information on the seriousness of moral transgressions through their speed and tone of response. Caregivers who talk to their children about incidences in a way that engages the child to consider the harm done to others and what others might be feeling helps them to learn to be concerned for others. Caregivers who do this have been found to have children who were more likely to engage in reparative behaviours (Zahn-Waxler *et al*, 1979). Managing this developmental task is a challenge for caregivers as they need to both down-regulate the child's emotion and also show disapproval.

Fonagy (2003) outlines the role of attachment in the development of theory of mind, empathy and a pro-social orientation, crucial for moral development. Empathy is required to develop a concern for others' well-being. In order for this to develop, children first need to develop a sense of "me" vs. "others" and have a mental representation of others' minds, which occurs through the development of theory of mind at around three years. Theory of mind enables children to think about what others are thinking and know that others are also thinking about what the child may be thinking (Baron-Cohen, 1991). Being able to infer the mental states of others is particularly important, because, as we get older, relying on external cues becomes more difficult because social norms encourage the minimisation of more explicit emotional expression. As well as acquiring the ability to infer what others might be thinking, in order to be able to effectively deploy empathy a child also requires the ability to employ effortful control of their emotions, in order to regulate emotions that are created by a concern for another's situation. This emotion regulation enables the child to focus their attention on the "other" rather than be overwhelmed by their own feelings. Such effortful control relies on the development of the pre-frontal cortex (Eisenberg, 2005), which, as outlined earlier, is still developing throughout adolescence. The development of emotion regulation is covered in more detail under the social cognition section later in this chapter, but secure attachments are crucial to learning how to self-regulate emotional states (Fonagy, 2003; Howe, 2011).

Research has consistently found a difference between offenders and non-offenders on moral reasoning (Nelson *et al*, 1990; Palmer, 2003), with offenders showing lower levels of moral reasoning than non-offenders. There have been a number of attempts to examine whether moral reasoning is linked to particular types of offending, but this has not provided consistent evidence for specificity in moral reasoning.

Conceptualising resilience

Resilience has been defined by Rutter (2006) as the 'relative resistance to environmental risk experiences . . . the overcoming of stress or adversity' (Rutter, 2006, p. 1). Other formulations of resilience emphasise the importance of the ability to face the future positively and having the capacity to meet future challenges (Masten, 2001). Defining resilience has moved on from describing it as an individual trait to an ability to recover from negative events, which can be promoted and enhanced. This shift is helpful as it implies that individuals can develop this ability with support and therefore provides hope for young people who have faced multiple adversities in their lives. Rutter (2006) has argued that it is important to think about resilience in relation to risk, as resilience occurs as a response to exposure to risk.

In developmental terms, graduated exposure to risk, as part of normal growing up and while supported by sensitive carers, can help to develop resilience as part of the promotion of positive adaptation. Olsson *et al* (2003) suggest that it is helpful to be clear whether resilience is being defined as an *outcome*, for example, functioning in everyday life despite exposure to risk, or a *process*, for example, what an individual is doing to cope with adverse circumstances. Outcomes approaches to resilience have tended to measure *mental health status, functional capacity* and *social competence* to evidence an individual's resilience, while process approaches have considered dynamic psychological activity to maintain resilience, such as *self-reflection* and using relationships to maintain *self-esteem* (Hauser *et al*, 2006). Rutter (2006) also proposes taking a life-span approach to considering resilience, as later life positive experiences can interrupt and divert the *downward spiral* that exposure to risk factors can trigger. He describes these positive experiences as '"turning points"'. An example Rutter gives from Laub and Sampson (2003) is marriage to a non-deviant peer enabling an individual to change their social networks, move away from a deprived area and change the way they spend their leisure time, indicating that turning point experiences are not just a result of one factor (in this case a secure attachment to the spouse) but are due to multiple positive factors and can occur in adulthood as well as childhood.

While the term resilience is conceptualised as residing within the individual, describing the individual's ability to resist the negative influences of risk experiences, it is also helpful to consider factors external to the individual that have been found to be protective for the individual to promote their resilience in the face of adverse circumstances known to be related to offending. Both these perspectives will be considered in reviewing the evidence.

Social cognition and resilience

Social cognition refers to an individual's abilities to recognise, understand and think about emotions in interpersonal and wider social contexts. Humans are social by nature and Oately (2004) outlines how we have evolved to be attuned to our own and each other's emotions and how this has proved functional for us as a species, allowing us to maximise the benefits of living co-operatively in groups. These emotion-based skills divide into intrapersonal and interpersonal domains. Intrapersonal skills include identifying how we feel and making sense of those feelings in relation to different social contexts and differing social norms. We also then have to develop the ability to self-regulate powerful emotions, again in relation to social context. Our ability to self-regulate emotion starts with our primary carer and attachment to that carer. Bowlby's (1969) attachment theory and subsequent research evidence has established the importance of developing a secure attachment to a carer and an important function of this attachment is the child using the carer in the co-regulation of their emotions. A good carer will be available, sensitive and reliable in order for the child to develop trust and feel secure enough to explore and learn new things. By helping the child in soothing powerful emotions, such as anger, the carer helps the child to develop their own strategies and provides organising principles for thinking about emotions.

The second domain of social cognition consists of including others in terms of emotion, such as recognising verbal, non-verbal and facial expressions of emotion in other people; thinking about what other people are feeling and thinking (theory of mind); and making decisions about how to behave based on this information (attribution). Masten (2004) highlights the importance of regulatory processes for developing resilience and suggests that while individuals will have resilience-based attributes, such as good intra- and interpersonal skills, they are also exposed to individuals, other than family, who can improve their resilience through assisting them to develop and improve such skills. Sometimes described as access to social capital (Sampson *et al*, 1997), social connections outside the family help provide a wider network of opportunity for young people, such as connections made through school, clubs and youth centres. Adults and peers in these settings offer opportunities for young people to learn about interpersonal skills in social contexts that extend beyond the home.

Emotion regulation

Research into emotions has examined both the biological nature of the basic emotions (happiness, sadness, fear, disgust and anger), which have been argued to be important for survival purposes of reproduction, risk avoidance, resource protection and disease prevention (Ekman, 1992; Plutchik, 1980), and the social functions of emotions, which help explain the more complex emotions such as guilt or embarrassment (Averill, 1980). It has been argued that emotions have evolved to form the foundations of social relationships (Oately and Jenkins, 1986; Keltner *et al*, 2006). The emotions of love, sexual desire and jealousy help individuals form and maintain attachments, and other emotions of gratitude, guilt, embarrassment, anger and envy help create and maintain co-operative relations with non-kin (Axelrod, 1984; Buss, 2000).

As emotions are experienced by individuals as instant and often perceived as uncontrollable, it has been suggested that they are therefore biologically driven phenomena, in that emotions are felt first and made conscious second (Zajonc, 1980). This issue has been extensively debated (Lazarus and Folkman, 1984), as the theoretical implication of biologically driven feelings is that individuals are less able to determine their actions. This view is what underpins the distinction between the legal terms of hot vs. cold blooded murder. Nonetheless, there are individuals who appear to be able to regulate their emotions better than others across contexts, which suggests that there is some individual control for managing social relationships constructively. In the West, emotions are socially constructed as unreliable and impulsive, and often contrasted with reason and rationality. The rational mind is favoured over what are perceived as uncontrollable biological emotional drives. This dichotomy in itself indicates that emotions can be experienced in both ways – they can sometimes feel overwhelming, but they can also be regulated.

In biological terms, there is evidence showing that both physiological and psychological mechanisms are involved in emotion production and processing. MacLean (1990), in his structural theory of the triune brain, argued that the brain has evolved into three distinct parts that are responsible for different functions. Broadly speaking, the striatal region or brain stem deals with motor activity, the control of metabolic systems, and the temporal rhythm of daily activities. The limbic system produces feelings and provides instant emotional responses to sensory information via the amygdala, which has been described by LeDoux (1993) as the primary appraisal mechanism for emotions in association with the hippocampus. The third part of MacClean's (1990) triune brain is the neocortex, which handles thought and planning. Although described structurally as separate, these systems work in parallel, with the limbic system able to overpower the cortex only in emergency situations to do with fight, flight or sexual reproduction (MacLean, 1990). During more routine everyday activity, speed of response is not the priority and the limbic system provides the cortex with evaluative information and the cortex helps give emotions meaning using context. Being able to understand emotions in this way is essential in order to maintain social relationships, as social hierarchies have to be remembered and opportunities for co-operation enhanced. This requires the ability to both reason about one's own emotions and identify what others are feeling, so that socially appropriate responses can be maximised. Physiological evidence of integrated working shows that brain activity between the limbic system and cortex is most active during social encounters (Frith and Frith, 2001).

Additional integration of brain function for effective emotional processing is required across the two hemispheres of the cortex. The right hemisphere controls non-verbal emotional processing, facial recognition and interpretation, and visual and spatial analyses. The left hemisphere controls language, logic, cause-and-effect thinking, calculation, analysis and reflection. The left hemisphere appears to have some inhibitory effect on the right hemisphere, as damage to the left side is associated with less inhibited behaviour and language, thus playing an important role for individual emotional self-control. Furthermore, the development of good neural pathways from childhood is necessary for emotional processing to be effective in later life. From early in life, neurological pathways are strengthened in areas that are stimulated, but reduced in areas that are not stimulated in response to experience in the external environment. Positive experiences for influencing emotional neurological pathways include forming secure attachments to primary caregivers, learning how to regulate strong emotions, and learning how to recognise and talk about emotions (Seigel, 1999). The biological structure and processes of emotion indicate that both emotion and reason are needed to effectively interact within social environments and to help individuals make sense of social encounters. It is the integration of emotion and reason that produces individuals who could currently be described as emotionally intelligent, in that they are able to identify and understand emotions in themselves and others, and they can reason about emotion to produce a range of behavioural options that allow them to manage their emotional responses.

As language has been found to be important for achieving emotion regulation, this ability also influences impulsive and aggressive behaviour. Language is increasingly important for young people as they grow up, as we use language to negotiate difficult situations; language therefore underpins important coping strategies. Young people who find it difficult to express themselves verbally can find themselves misinterpreted and labelled as "difficult" (Sanger *et al*, 2001). Offenders have been found to have less language knowledge (Bryan *et al*, 2007), but interventions rarely address the speech and language difficulties faced by young offenders.

Restorative justice and social cognition

Restorative justice, defined as 'a process whereby parties with a stake in a specific offence collectively resolve how to deal with the aftermath of the offence and its implications for the future' (Marshall, 1999, p. 5) has become an increasingly popular process for responding to youth crime ranging from shoplifting and burglary to offences against the person.

Braithwaite (1989, p. 12) proposed that offenders would be most affected by "reintegrative shaming" from their own communities. He suggested that, while shaming might cause offenders to feel stigmatised and cause them to offend more, reintegrating shaming relied on the offenders' need of approval and support from their own community and networks. Being encouraged to do better by the offender's own supportive social groups might have a more lasting impact on their behaviour. Wachtel (1999a) further expanded this idea by adopting Baumrind's (1989) theory to illustrate that restorative justice would be most effective if the processes offered high support and high control when working with offenders, similar to good parenting.

Zehr (2002) suggested that crime was 'a violation of people and interpersonal relationships' and the purpose of restorative justice was to 'repair harm' made to these connections (Zehr and Mika, 2002, p. 64). Restorative justice, therefore, encourages offenders to have face-to-face interactions with their victims and communities in the hope that hearing about the victim's experience will cause offenders to feel shame, guilt and empathy, and, in turn, encourage behavioural changes. Both shame and guilt have been linked to increased levels of empathy and the desire to make reparations (Brown and Cehajic, 2008) and role-taking exercises have been seen to be effective in increasing empathy. Because of the process's links to models of effective parenting, restorative justice has been increasingly used not only as a response to criminal events but also to prevent crime and improve social cohesion in institutions responsible for the socialisation of children, such as schools (Wachtel, 1999b) and residential units.

In simple terms, restorative justice is about storytelling (Umbreit, 1998). Any empathy, shame or guilt experienced by the participants is brought on through the direct exchange of experiences by the victim and the offender. The ability to tell stories has been recognised as a fundamental way of making social connections (Riessman, 2008) and to be integral to the organisation of memory (Mandler, 1984). Restorative justice, therefore, inadvertently tests offenders' abilities to tell coherent stories. For this reason, restorative justice has also been described as tense meetings where 'verbal accounts . . . are scrutinised and assessed by other participants, whose own accounts are in turn scrutinised' (Roche, 2006, pp. 79–80).

The reality of restorative justice may be that the participants, who include a potentially traumatised victim as well as a young offender with a possible history of disadvantage and trauma, are asked not only to tell their own stories coherently but also to determine the truthfulness of the accounts they hear. This will be particularly difficult for young offenders with emotional developmental delay. There remains, however, optimism about the possibilities of restorative justice for vulnerable young people, to the degree it has been described as '*offender*-specific programming', capable of being tailored to the individual needs of all participants (Verrecchia, 2009) and therefore providing an opportunity for developing the skills of mentalisation.

Adaptive emotion management

For emotion to function adaptively to facilitate social relationships, individuals need to be able to communicate their emotional state visually and audibly as well as recognise emotional states in others. Paul Ekman has been foremost in the establishment of discrete universal categories of facial expression of emotion (Keltner and Ekman, 2000). Most evidence exists for the five core emotions (Plutchik, 2001): anger, fear, happiness, sadness and surprise. The importance of recognising emotion expression for creating empathetic response has been well documented in Theory of Mind research linked to the function of "mirror" neurons, which appear to facilitate imitation and stimulate similar emotional responses upon perceiving emotions in others, for example, quickening of the heart upon seeing fear on another's face (Keysers and Gazzola, 2006). Other empirical work has shown that facial expression, vocal tone and other non-verbal cues can be differentially recognised (Mayer *et al*, 1990; Johnstone and Scherer, 2000). The ability to identify and attend to physiological arousal, discriminate between feeling states and reflect on emotional events helps individuals to build complex emotional self schemas and knowledge about the significance of each emotion and how they work together and sequentially. Such knowledge has been found to give individuals a better chance for choosing adaptive behaviours. Lane and Pollerman (2002) argue for a similar process of emotional development in line with Piaget's (1976) theory of cognitive development, whereby an individual's awareness of their own actions and reactions is constructed through cognitive processes and meta-cognition.

The creation of emotional schemas depends on the ability to represent feeling states and events symbolically, which is achieved through language. Verbalising emotional experiences facilitates conscious awareness of emotions and enables the differentiation and co-ordination of emotional experiences into abstract emotional concepts, which are accepted as the convention within the particular cultural context. Such reflective abstraction allows individuals to create knowledge, make deductions and inferences about emotions, and process emotional experiences more objectively, as such meta-cognition usually happens after the experience. Nonetheless, as knowledge develops, it is argued that the existence of more complex emotional representational schemas interacts with sensorimotor arousal during emotional encounters as well, giving an individual more behavioural response options.

Emotional schemas include knowledge about what the feeling is like in terms of how the body reacts; how the emotion looks outwardly; what usually causes that feeling; what factors usually enhance or reduce the feeling; what behaviours are usually associated with the feeling; and what the socially appropriate responses are depending on context. Lane and Schwartz (1987) proposed a model to outline the developmental stages of emotional awareness, indicating in ascending order that at level 1 an individual would be aware of physical sensations; at level 2 they would be aware of their action tendencies, i.e. what they feel like doing, for example, punching a wall; at level 3 there would be an awareness of discrete emotions; at level 4 there would be an awareness of blends of emotions, for example, love being a blend of joy and trust (Plutchik, 2001); and finally at level 5, an individual would be aware of blends of emotions or the capacity to appreciate complexity and apparent contradiction in the experience of emotions, for example, a young person feeling anger and relief on the late arrival of a carer to pick them up from school.

The development of social cognition over the life course

Much of the emotion development literature mirrors attachment theory principles in children's development of reciprocity in inter-personal interactions, mind-mindedness and the creation of internal working models. In terms of social competence development in children, Harris and Saarni (1989) propose a model that includes biological/ temperamental factors as well as interpersonal and situational influences. They also outline a number of key social competencies that children develop. According to Harris and Saarni's model, emotional and social development in infancy depends primarily on biological responses; however, biological feelings interact with the social context. For example, neural connections are made as children associate their own emotions with emotion expressions on others' faces. Children learn to link what they feel with what facial expressions look like when other people feel sad. Parents help model this basic emotion under-standing for infants by mirroring their expressions. From the age of two, children develop ways of using emotion as communication and develop emotional schemas that allow them to anticipate events and achieve simple social goals. From the age of six to adolescence, young people gradually develop more complex and abstract ways of thinking about emotion and use emotion to achieve more complex social goals. Their emotional vocabulary and cultural knowledge of emotional norms and rules develop. They also start to reflect on their own emotion experiences and have some insight into their own emotion traits (Harris and Saarni, 1989).

Bannerjee (2003) concurs with Harris and Saarni's model, but suggests three phases of social development in children. Very young children, up to five years old, develop a basic understanding of emotion and seek situational explanations for expressed emotions (e.g. the girl is crying because she fell over) and explore the conse-quences of expressed emotions. The second phase involves children developing an internal mental schema about emotions, particularly an understanding that their emotional representations remembered from past events can also contribute to how they feel as well as the trigger of an external event (Bannerjee, 2003). These competencies appear to develop alongside developing theory of mind in young children from three years and older, but these competencies are more effective in older children from nine and older. Bannerjee's third phase describes children developing an understanding of cultural emotion norms, strategies for emotional self-regulation, and knowledge of inter-personal consequences.

Emotion self-regulation is an important skill to learn for children, particularly as they enter adolescence and experience greater expect-ations placed upon them by adults, at a time when they are interacting more and more with the external world. Gross and Thompson (2007) outline five characteristics of emotion self-regulation, which we describe below. Firstly, individuals can plan ahead and think about situations which might be problematic, thus allowing them to think about ways in which such situations could be avoided or modified. Such planning can help give an individual more of a sense of agency and control. Secondly, once in any given situation, an individual can think about ways in which the situation could be modified, such as changing an appointment time. Thirdly, an individual can use their attention in different ways, either to distract themselves from upsetting events or by concentrating on the emotional features of a situation. Fourthly, changing how one appraises a situation can influence how one feels about it, and finally, individuals can attempt to control their response to a situation, such as using exercise to channel aggression or anxiety, or using drugs and alcohol to dampen feelings (Gross and Thompson, 2007). Emotion self-regulation depends largely on the ability to think about emotions in relation to one's own reactions and also in relation to social norms. Individuals who have been encouraged in childhood to think about what they are feeling, to attribute several causes and think about alternative responses to feelings are better prepared to deal with life's adversities, as they have developed a wider range of mental strategies to help them cope. Bannerjee (2003) indicates that as children develop they move from an external approach to emotion self-regulation, for instance, thinking about changing the *situation itself* compared to a more internal approach, such as changing the way they *think about* a situation. Research into emotion self-regulation and offending indicates that young people with poor emotion regulation are associated with reactive aggression type behaviours, a type of aggression that is spontaneous, emotionally charged and a defensive reaction to a perceived threat (Mullin and Hinshaw, 2007).

In terms of emotion expression, there appears to be a developmental pattern. Babies have been found to show an attentional preference for faces and also an *attentional* bias for fear expressions. It is argued that this bias has an adaptive function in that fear expressions signal a threat, although in order to make most use of the fear signal, children have to develop theory of mind, to put themselves in another's shoes in order to interpret what might be causing the fear expression (Skuse, 2003). The *recognition* of emotion expressions takes place later as children develop categorical labels for emotions. While very young children (as young as seven months) have been shown to be able to distinguish between fear and anger expressions (Leppänen, 2011), it is not until infants develop language that we can assess their accuracy in distinguishing between categories of emotion. The first distinctions that are recognised are the dichotomy of happy/ unhappy, followed by distinguishing between happy, angry and sad and then fear and surprise. Anger expressions indicate an immediate threat to the self and therefore are an expression that is recognised earlier in children's development than fear. Recognising happy, angry and sad (in that order) occurs from the age of two years onwards (Widen and Russell, 2007), while the ability to recognise fear seems to occur by about four to five years. It is argued that biological responses (autonomic nervous system, hormonal changes, central nervous system) reflect differential metabolic changes for positive and negative emotions; however, the evidence for *specific* biological responses for emotion states, e.g. anger, fear, is not strong (see Lewis (2011) for a review). Therefore it appears that, in order to help children make sense of emotional states, it is important to develop children's knowledge of cultural categories of emotion through language (Skuse, 2003) to develop their ability to interpret social cues, manage their own emotional responses and understand the social consequences of particular types of behaviour, such as aggression.

Social information processing

In the same bio-social tradition as Harris and Saarni (1989) and Bannerjee (2003), Dodge and Petit (2003) outlined a bio-psychosocial model showing the development of chronic conduct disorder, which encompasses social information processing of the kind that Saarni and Bannerjee describe (see Figure 1). Dodge and Petit's model shows the mediating influences of parenting on the biological predispositions of the adolescent and peer influence on the socio-cultural context. They argue that parenting has the most important influence inter-acting with biological predisposition *early on* in the child's develop-ment, but that peer influence has more influence in association with the sociocultural context as the child becomes an *adolescent.*

Figure 1
A bio-psychosocial model of the development of conduct disorder in adolescence (Dodge and Petit, 2003)

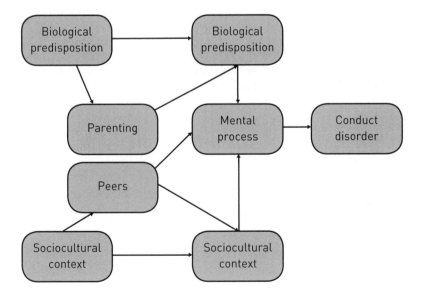

Crick and Dodge (1994) developed a specific model of social information processing, which represents the mental processes box in the
conduct disorder model shown in Figure 1. Using a cognitive information processing approach, they propose specific stages that individuals go through when processing social cues (see Figure 2). These
stages involve first encoding the social cues where the individual
attends to the relevant ones. In the second stage they interpret these
cues, using their mental schema or internal working model, which
guides them as to whether to interpret the cue as benign or hostile in
intent. The third phase involves a search for possible responses to the
cue, which will depend on each individual's experiences which will
have been stored in memory. Possible responses are evaluated in
Stage 4 and behaviour ensues in Stage 5. Crick and Dodge (1994) warn
that although the process is described as linear, they acknowledge the
evidence from neuroscience, which shows that such information
processing is more likely to happen in parallel rather than in series,
but for purposes of understanding each step it is easier to explain the
process in a linear manner. None of these processes is necessarily
conscious and multiple sets of processing will be occurring in any
social situation.

Figure 2
Social information processing stages

Stage 1	• Encoding social cues
Stage 2	• Interpretation of cues
Stage 3	• Response search
Stage 4	• Response evaluation
Stage 5	• Enactment/behaviour

In Stage 1 an individual perceives and codes the social information, such as verbal, non-verbal and emotion expression type cues, which are available from any social situation that they pay attention to. There will be individual differences in what they pay attention to, known as attentional bias. In the second stage, these cues will be interpreted by the individual and judged to be positive, neutral or negative to the individual's well-being. Interpretation of social cues will vary across individuals depending upon their experience, which will have influenced their neural associative networks. For example, someone who has experienced physical abuse is likely to interpret anger in an expression more often than an individual who has not. If they are to respond to the social cue, the individual has to think of a number of possible responses and evaluate these possibilities as to the most appropriate (as they see it), and once selected, the individual enacts the response.

Evidence for social information processing models

Encoding social cues

There has been extensive empirical work carried out in testing these social information processing models in children, particularly in relation to social information processing deficits and outcomes. There is consistent evidence showing that deficits in social information processing predict aggressive behaviour (Dodge *et al*, 1986; Denham and Bouril, 1994). In terms of deficits at Stage 1, the encoding of social cues, men who are persistent violent offenders and diagnosed with psychopathic traits are poor at recognising fear and sadness and respond more to reward than punishment (Dadds *et al*, 2006; Munoz, 2009). These trends have also been identified in boys who show callous-unemotional traits, which predict psychopathy in adulthood (Patrick, 2006). While the presence of callous-unemotional traits appears to be linked to poor fear recognition, groups of boys who have experienced physical abuse in their developmental years show hypersensitivity to anger in face recognition studies (Pollack *et al*, 2000) and other studies have shown a link between anger recognition bias and problem classroom behaviours (Barth and Bastiani, 1997). Similarly, boys with conduct disorder, and who do not show callous-unemotional traits, display impulsivity and reactive aggression and perceive hostility in even neutral faces. This conduct disorder group has lower than average verbal ability, which contrasts to the callous-unemotional traits group, which shows higher levels of IQ (Frick and Marsee, 2006). The conduct disorder group, however, does respond well to parenting interventions.

Interpretation bias

In Dodge *et al*'s study (1986), in comparison to average children, aggressive children had deficits at each of the five social information processing stages, but in provocation situations it was the *interpretation* stage (stage 2) which most predicted an aggressive response. Dodge *et al* (1995) showed that social information processing mediated the effect of physical abuse on later conduct problems, specifically the stages of encoding social cues and accessing responses, stages 1 and 3. Children who have experienced neglect show difficulties in discriminating between negative emotions (Pollack *et al*, 2000), but it would appear that it is young people who have experienced physical abuse who are more likely to have anti-social behaviour problems (Grogan-Kaylor *et al*, 2008). This link has also been shown in studies that have also controlled for socio-economic status (SES) and ethnicity (Dodge *et al*, 1995).

However, the link between having experienced physical abuse and enacting aggressive behaviour is not a given; Widom and Maxfield (1996) showed that this link can be buffered by stable out-of-home care for young people who had entered care as a result of abuse or neglect (e.g. foster care). This suggests that good quality caregiving could provide opportunities for a young person to change their social information processing style. This proposition is supported by neuro-cognition studies which show that, although there are periods of development that appear sensitive to forming perception and interpretation of social cues, the plasticity (adaptability) of the brain allows for the occurrence of changes in social information processing. However, changing established patterns of social information processing is likely to take longer than when establishing new patterns, as two processes need to occur: behaviour based on established neural pathways needs to be discouraged and alternative behaviour encouraged to develop new pathways, compared to the single process of strengthening new pathways for behaviour in young infants (Leppänen, 2011).

Extensive work on hostile attribution bias (stage 2), where the individual is asked to provide reasons for the intent of another's action, provides consistent evidence of the link between hostile attribution bias and aggressive behaviour. Studies show that this effect holds across actual and hypothetical situations, across normative and clinical populations (Crick and Dodge, 1994). However, hostile attribution bias is only associated with reactive interpersonal aggression. It does not operate for proactive aggression where teasing or bullying is involved, nor for aggression towards objects. Also hostile attribution bias has been tested across a number of commonly experienced situations for young people: provocation, group entry, object acquisition and friendship initiation situations (see Crick and Dodge (1994) for a review). Moderating factors for social information processing and aggressive behaviour include gender and age. Boys show more physical and verbal aggression than girls, who show more indirect aggression designed to harm interpersonal relationships. There are not many studies assessing the effect of gender as a moderator of social information processing on behaviour, possibly as fewer girls are included in studies on aggressive behaviour. However, Crick and Dodge (1994) hypothesise that for behaviour that is atypical for the gender, e.g. hitting in girls, social information processing deficits are likely to be at the extreme end of a normative distribution for their gender. In terms of age, as the normal developmental course is for children to become less aggressive as they get older, children with aggressive behaviours tend to be developmentally behind in their social information processing skills (Dodge et al, 1995; Conduct Problems Prevention Research Group, 2002).

In summary, emotional development is essential to the development of social information processing skills and it is particularly important that this development occurs within the first five years of life. Although social information processing deficits can occur in young people, these can be buffered by good quality and stable care and peer acceptance for most young people, with the exception of those who show callous-unemotional traits. Social information processing is linked to reactive interpersonal aggression, particularly for emotion recognition, hostile attribution bias (interpretation of intent) and response access. Such processing is also a mediator of the influence of physical abuse on the development of aggressive behaviour.

Known risk and resilience factors for offending

Risk and resilience factors can be usefully grouped according to Bronfenbrenner's (1979) ecosystem model showing the differential influences of variables, depending upon their context, on individual characteristics, such as intelligence or hyperactivity, family-related risk factors such as parental drug use, school-based risk factors such as truancy, and community-based risk factors such as prevalence of criminal activity where an individual lives. From reviews and meta-analyses of risk factors for offending, we have produced a compilation of these in Tables 1 to 7 below under these headings: individual, family, education and community.[2]

Individual risk and resilience factors

Many of the risks associated with offending at an individual level have been outlined above. However, it is through the display of emotional and behavioural difficulties at a young age that many young people

---

[2] These tables were compiled from evidence from the following authors: Farrington, 1978; Furstenberg et al, 1987; Morash and Rucker, 1989; Bebbington and Miles, 1989; Hawkins et al, 1992; Utting et al, 1993; Farrington, 1995; Hope, 1996; Bottoms and Wiles, 1997; Hawkes et al, 1997; Lipsey and Derzon, 1998; Patterson et al, 1998; Dean and Hastings, 2000; Loeber and Farrington, 2000; Cottle et al, 2001; Masten, 2001; Moffit and Caspi, 2001; Aber et al, 2003; Brennan et al, 2003; Dent and Jowitt, 2003; Hagell, 2003; Wiig et al, 2003; NACRO, 2005; Borum and Verhaagen, 2006; Ryan et al, 2008; Leschied et al, 2008; Murray, 2009; Dicataldo et al, 2009.

become involved in anti-social behaviour and then offending, and these difficulties are described below.

There is a wide interdisciplinary range of literature on emotional and behavioural difficulties in young people, all with differing definitions of abnormal behaviour. We outline some of the key terms used here. There is a distinction between externalising and internalising behaviours (Achenbach, 1978). Externalising disorders are defined as children's behaviour that can be observed where the child acts negatively on the *external* environment. Externalising behaviours fall into aggressive, hyperactive and delinquent categories. Internalising disorders are defined as behaviours where the child is withdrawn, anxious, inhibited and depressed, affecting the child's *internal* psychological environment rather than the external world. In reality it is recognised that these categories are not completely distinct and that many children with externalising problems will also suffer from internalising problems as well.

The constructs of aggression, hyperactivity and delinquency can be further defined as follows. Aggressive behaviour has been defined by the American Psychiatric Association (APA) as: 'physical or verbal behaviours that harm or threaten to harm others, including children, adults and animals' (APA, 1994). Aggression can be further divided into reactive aggression and proactive aggression. Reactive aggression has been characterised as impulsive, spontaneous and emotional, whereas proactive aggression is more intentional and planned and often involves teasing or bullying (Dodge, 1991). As outlined previously, early onset of aggressive behaviours has been found to have a strong link to later offending (Farrington, 1991).

Hyperactivity refers to two main types of dysfunction: displaying an excess of motor activity, restlessness and impulsivity, and displaying attention deficits, particularly being unable to sustain and adjust attention in a controlled setting. The Diagnostic and Statistical Manual of Mental Disorders (DSM-IV) allows for three sub-types of hyperactivity: mostly hyperactivity, mostly attention deficit and a combination of both (APA, 1994). The formal diagnosis of hyperactivity comes under the category of Attention Deficit Hyperactivity Disorder (ADHD).

Delinquency is a broad term and it has been used in narrow terms to indicate law breaking as well as in a wider context to indicate anti-social acts such as theft, burglary, robbery, vandalism, drug use and violence and, as such, is similar to offending.

Conduct disorder is a term used in the mental health context to encapsulate externalising behaviours to the extent that these behaviours have become repetitive, show a persistent pattern, and are causing disruption to social and educational functioning. However, conduct disorder includes a slightly wider range of disruptive behaviours, including aggression to people or animals, the destruction of property, theft and/or deceitfulness and serious violations of rules (APA, 1994). As with externalising disorders, early onset conduct disorder predicts later persistent offending and late onset adolescent limited offending in accordance with Moffitt's (1993) typology.

The types of biological predisposition for conduct disorder include genetic factors of levels of impulsivity, attention and temperament

Table 1
Individual risk factors associated with offending

Anti-social behaviour
Aggressive behaviour; oppositional defiant disorder; conduct disorder; history of violence; in trouble with police from young age; substance use

Impulsivity
Difficulty concentrating; motor restlessness; hyperactivity; attention seeking

Mental health
Depressive symptoms; anxiety

Self-worth
More likely to experience low expectations; more likely to experience low encouragement; few opportunities to feel worthwhile; few opportunities to feel needed; limited personal resources

Age
Adolescent limited (normal part of adolescence; late onset of offending); life course offenders (psychopathic tendencies; early onset of offending); risk factors identified at older age, greater risk of crime as adult

(Cadoret *et al*, 1995; Miles and Carey, 1997) and chemical imbalances due to substance use in pregnancy (deCubas and Field, 1993). These genetic factors tend to predict dysregulated behaviour rather than violent behaviour, but children who find it difficult to negotiate everyday life are more at risk of violent behaviours. It is also the combinations and interactions of genes that appear to be influential rather than genes on their own (Rutter and Silberg, 2002).

Table 2
Individual resilience factors associated with resistance to offending

Self-regulation – skills for emotion and behaviour
Self-worth – feeling positive about oneself
Hopefulness – positive outlook
Self-efficacy – feeling competent
Appealing qualities – talents, skills, ability to engage
Cognitive abilities – attention and problem-solving skills

Family risk and resilience factors

Among the socio-cultural influences on conduct disorder are socio-economic circumstances that the child is born into, such as the income, occupation and education of parents (Bradley and Corwyn, 2002). Parental divorce (Amato, 2001), interparental conflict (Davies and Windle, 2001), being born to teenage parents (Morash and Rucker, 1989) and being part of a single-parent family (Ackerman *et al*, 2001) have also been shown to be associated with higher levels of conduct disorder. Parenting mediators of biological predispositions include harsh parenting, physical abuse (Wiig *et al*, 2003; Ryan and Testa, 2005; Leschied *et al*, 2008), and lack of warmth (McFadyen-Ketchum *et al*, 1996), particularly if these are experienced before the age of five years.

Table 3
Family risk factors

Family structure

Teenage parent; single-parent family; in care – lower threshold for reporting offending behaviour of those in care

Resources

Limited material resources; poverty (in receipt of benefits)

Parent's mental health

From families experiencing stressful life events; mother's poor mental health

Negative parental influence

Other family members known to the police; parental drug and alcohol abuse; coerciveness; authoritarian style; harsh punitive parenting; lack of child supervision; inconsistent parenting; no reliable consistent carer; parental conflict; witnessing violence between caregivers

Abuse and neglect

Physical abuse; emotional abuse; neglect – physical and emotional; sexual abuse; chronic maltreatment (continuous throughout childhood and adolescence leads to greater risk)

Family relationships

Distanced from family; history of family dysfunction; poor relationship with parents

Table 4
Family resilience factors

Secure attachment – to caregiver

Authoritative parenting – providing affection, monitoring, expectations, setting boundaries

Bonds – with other positive adults (family, friends, mentors, teachers, professionals)

Socio-economic advantages – adequate, reliable income

Education risk and resilience factors

Risk factors within the education realm specifically for offending also predict poor outcomes for education achievement and subsequent employment. Young people displaying early signs of ADHD or impulsive behaviours struggle with attention and concentration as school becomes more demanding (Dicataldo *et al*, 2009). Poor impulse control is also connected to aggressive responses to peers as navigating social situations also becomes more complex with age (Leschied *et al*, 2008). Low IQ has been found to be linked to offending (Farrington, 1995) and low attainment (Borum and Verhaagen, 2006). Exclusion from school is associated with offending and school exclusions are often due to challenging behaviour (Osler *et al*, 2001). Schools provide the first avenue into wider social networks and complex social interactions bound by social norms and institutional rules; they are the first key societal institution, independent of the family, within which children have to learn to interact effectively. Children who are excluded from this environment not only miss out on formal education opportunities, but also on important socialising processes that help young people to understand how to effectively manage the adult world within a supported environment.

Table 5
Education risk and resilience factors

Education risk factors
Learning difficulties (SEN); school exclusion; low IQ; low school achievement

Education resilience factors
School bonding; school effectiveness; school attendance; learning and problem-solving skills; opportunities to develop skills and talents

Community risk and resilience factors

Developing relationships with peers is a key identity activity for adolescent development. As adolescents are becoming more independent from family influence and determining their own identity, they seek confirmation and validation from peers. As social networks widen, social identity becomes more important as adolescents learn about social norms and the importance of conformity for group membership (Coleman, 2011). Adolescents can achieve this psychological development by associating with both positive and negative peers. The attraction of delinquent peers is that they often show independence from adult authority and are more likely to take part in adult behaviours early, such as driving, drug and alcohol use and sex. Brown (2004) indicates that peers provide different forms of influence: firstly, through providing models of behaviour that other young people can aspire to; secondly, by providing opportunities for activities; and thirdly, by providing a forum for normative regulation where young people can talk about what is right and wrong.

Contact with aggressive peers (Sinclair *et al*, 1994) and early social rejection from peers (Laird *et al*, 2001) have been linked to offending. Patterson *et al* (1998) suggest that it is the double risk of disrupted parenting and association with delinquent peers that is most likely to predict chronic offending.

As outlined in the social cognition and resilience section above, young people who show good emotion regulation abilities are less likely to be aggressive (Nagin and Tremblay, 2001). Fonagy (2003) provides a useful summary of the important links between attachment, acquiring mentalisation skills (the ability to think about what others are thinking) and emotion regulation in curbing violence and aggression. Losel and Bliesener (1994) examined two groups of high-risk adolescents and compared the characteristics of those who had developed conduct problems with those who had not. They found that the resilient group were more intelligent, were more flexible and had a positive self-concept. They perceived themselves as more competent and were proactive in seeking opportunities and were more forward looking. Masten's (2001) study supports this and adds that resilient individuals had strong connections with one or more effective parents, had positive bonds with other adults, and connections with positive and competent peers. Resilient individuals were also more likely to have connections with positive organisations, such as clubs or faith groups, and lived in areas that were safe and provided opportunities to be involved with positive organisations.

Gilligan (2000, 2009) outlined a rationale for the benefits of positive spare-time experiences for young people in care, which included the establishment of routine, self-discipline and a sense of purpose; providing opportunities to meet positive peers and adults and widen social networks; providing opportunities to belong to constructive social groups; and developing self-efficacy. Unsupervised time away from home has been found to be associated with offending (Flannery et al, 1999). Feldman and Matjasko (2005) found in their review of research on the impact of extracurricular activities on a number of adolescent outcomes, including delinquency, that involvement in activities is positive, but that this is less clear once moderator variables are introduced. For example, certain activities such as sports participation appear to be associated with some negative outcomes such as alcohol use (Eccles et al, 2003).

Table 6
Community risk factors

Housing
Social housing; high turnover of residents

Neighbourhood
Deprived neighbourhood; densely populated areas; vandalism, fly-tipping, graffiti; low or erratic police presence; high unemployment

Community opportunities
Minimal organised community activity; opportunities to offend; community crime and violence

Peers
Opportunity to associate with delinquent peers; friends who engage in risky activities

Table 7
Community resilience factors

Community opportunities	
Involvement in positive activity; opportunities to develop skills and talents; bonding and connections to positive organisations (clubs, faith groups); opportunities for regulatory capacity-building	
Neighbourhood	
Quality of the community (safety, presence of positive organisations); socio-economic advantages	
Peers	
Association with pro-social and competent peers	

Interaction of risk factors

In the review of the literature for the development of their model, Crick and Dodge (1994) argue that multiple risk factors within this model increase risk, but that this may not be a linear function but a curvilinear pattern, such that at above a certain threshold of risk the probability of conduct disorder accelerates. For example, Aber *et al* (2003) showed that the likelihood of hostile attribution bias and aggressive interpersonal strategies accelerated upwards from 12 years from a relatively flat linear pattern between the ages of 7.5 years and 12 years. Thelen (2001) also found that within the normal range of harsh parenting there was no effect on conduct disorder but that this increased when harsh parenting became physical abuse. Also there are interactions between variables that can *buffer* the development of conduct disorder; peer acceptance and friendship buffers the effects of family adversity, socio-economic status, exposure to marital conflict, and harsh discipline (Dodge and Petit, 2003).

Interactions between biological predispositions and parenting environment were examined by Cloninger *et al* (1982) using adoption data in a twin study. They found that the combination of the criminality of biological parents and quality of adoptive parents interacted such that those children with non-criminal parents and low-risk adoptive parents had three per cent probability of conduct disorder; those with non-criminal parents and high-risk adoptive parents had

Table 8
Risk factors highlighted in meta-analyses of offending

Risk Factors	Lipsey and Derzon (1998) Retrospective longitudinal research	Cottle et al (2001) Risk of re-offending	Lesheid et al (2008) Prospective longitudinal research
Individual	Aggressive behaviour before age 12	Conduct problems	Aggressive behaviour
	A history of general offences	Young age at first offence	
	Impulsiveness		Difficulty concentrating
			Motor restlessness
			Attention seeking
		Stress and anxiety	Anxiety
			Depressive symptoms
Family	Anti-social parents	Family instability	Witnessing inter-parent conflict
		Physical/sexual abuse	Coercive/ authoritarian parenting
		Low socio-economic status	
		More out-of-home placements	Lack of child supervision
Education		Special Educational Need	
		Low academic achievement	
Community	Delinquent peers	Delinquent peers	
		Unconstructive use of leisure time	

seven per cent probability; those with criminal parents and low-risk adoptive parents had a 12 per cent probability; and those with the double dose of criminal parents and high-risk adoptive parents were 40 per cent more likely to have conduct disorder. These findings show that genetic factors and parenting environment can contribute protective elements against conduct disorder (Cloninger *et al*, 1982).

Relative importance of risk factors

Meta-analyses are studies that take several previous studies on a topic and synthesise the results to see which effects are statistically consistent and as such give us an idea of which factors might be most important for any given outcome. In the area of risk and offending, a number of meta-analyses are compared in Table 8.

Interventions need to address both types of risk at these multiple levels, but they also need to be aware of a different risk focus at different ages, for example, targeting family and school-related risks issues at an early age compared with providing stable adult relation-ships and constructive activity in adolescence. For young people in care, therapeutic interventions may be needed at any stage.

Summary

Risk

- Risks for offending appear to be particularly influential when they are cumulative and occur early in a young person's life.
- However, because of continued brain development in adolescence, risks can still be mitigated in adolescence by providing extra support to ensure that education and training opportunities are taken advantage of.
- When assessing risk, the following issues need to be considered:
  - Frequency – has the individual been exposed to multiple risk factors?
  - Type of risk – is the risk acute or chronic? Is the risk static or dynamic?
  - Timing – has the individual been exposed to risks at a young

age? Is the risk factor more problematic at certain times or in certain contexts?

- Source of risk – where does the risk originate from?

Risk factors

- Individual risk factors associated with offending include anti-social behaviour at a young age, impulsivity, mental health issues, low self-worth and age (late identification).
- Family-related risk factors include family breakdown, few resources, parental mental health difficulties, negative parental influence, abuse and neglect, and poor family relationships.
- Education risk factors include learning difficulties (SEN), school exclusion, low IQ and low school achievement.
- Community risk factors include poor housing, deprived neighbourhood, few community opportunities and association with delinquent peers.

Resilience

- Resilience occurs in response to negative events or experiencing risk and is the ability to recover from negative events. Individuals who have experienced negative events have been found to have "turning points" in later life after experiencing positive events, such as getting married or gaining employment.
- Emotion regulation is an important skill which is most effectively learned early in development to coincide with brain development; caregivers are crucial to help young people regulate their emotions, although the presence of other positive relationships outside the family can also help young people learn this skill.
- Developing an emotion vocabulary and way of thinking about emotionally charged situations helps young people develop their language skills and abstract thinking skills. Individuals who have been encouraged in childhood to think about what they are feeling, to attribute several causes and think about alternative responses to feelings are better prepared to deal with life's adversities, as they have developed a wider range of mental strategies to help them cope.

- Social information processing models describe in detail these skills. Emotional development is essential to the development of social information processing skills and it is particularly important that this development occurs within the first five years of life. Although social information processing deficits can occur in young people, these can be buffered by good quality and stable care and peer acceptance for most young people, with the exception of young people who show callous-unemotional traits. Social information processing is linked to reactive interpersonal aggression, particularly for emotion recognition, hostile attribution bias (interpretation of intent) and response access. Social information processing is also a mediator of the influence of physical abuse on the development of aggressive behaviour.

Resilience and protective factors

- Individual protective factors for offending include self-regulation, self-worth, hopefulness, self-efficacy, appealing qualities, and cognitive abilities.
- Family-related protective factors for offending include positive attachment to caregiver, authoritative parenting (providing affection, monitoring, expectations, setting boundaries) and bonds with other positive adults, and socio-economic advantages.
- Educational protective factors include school bonding, effective school, school attendance, learning and problem-solving skills, and opportunities to develop skills and talents.
- Community protective factors include non-deprived neighbourhood with community opportunities, such as safety, presence of positive organisations and opportunity to mix with pro-social peers.

4 Policy, procedure and practice: findings from the national survey and focus groups

This chapter brings together findings from the national survey of England and Wales and the four multi-agency focus groups.

The *national survey* (England and Wales) of Youth Offending Teams (YOTs) and LAC services mapped practice, procedure and approaches to working with looked after children who were at risk of offending across the full range of urban/rural geographic areas and local authority types. The questionnaires were designed to investigate key areas that affect care and youth offending pathways, e.g. local authority strategies and targets; preventative work; the use of restorative justice; the role of different placements (residential/foster care); working relationships between LAC and YOT workers; and perceptions of the contribution of other agencies (police, CPS, education, and health).

We piloted and discussed the questionnaires with YOT and LAC managers and practitioners. It was clear from the piloting feedback and these discussions that specific information and opinions needed to be drawn from different parts of each organisation. For example, as we wanted detail on preventative work as well as other interventions relevant to LAC children, it was decided to target a specific questionnaire at the YOS prevention teams. Similarly, in relation to LAC children, as we wanted to know more about the specific role of residential care and leaving care, we needed to target those working most directly in that area.

Six questionnaires were finally agreed for key staff: the head of YOS; the head of prevention services within YOS; the local authority manager responsible for looked after children's services; a team manager for looked after children; the manager responsible for leaving care services; and the manager responsible for residential services. The questionnaires were completed electronically, either online, or as a word file that was returned by email, or printed out and returned by post.

There was an overall response rate of 65 per cent (n = 113) for local authorities, with a 41 per cent (n = 72) response rate for at least one YOT questionnaire returned and a 45 per cent (n = 79) response rate for the return of at least one LAC questionnaire. The response rates for each postholder questionnaire are listed below.

YOT Head of Service	37%	(n = 64)
YOT Prevention Service Manager	24%	(n = 42)
LAC Service Manager	27%	(n = 47)
LAC Team Manager	21%	(n = 37)
LAC Residential Manager	21%	(n = 37)
LAC Leaving care Manager	25%	(n = 44)

There was some variation between regions in the level of response (with the exception of one region) from a low of 33 per cent to a high of 93 per cent, but we had representation from over 50 per cent for each region, suggesting a reasonable range of authorities with at least one questionnaire response within almost all regions and roughly even representation by type of authority.

Four focus groups were held with multi-agency professionals working with looked after children and offenders in each of the four local authorities used to recruit the sample of young people – one London borough, one northern city and two shire counties. Focus groups followed the framework of topics used in the national survey and were used to explore the survey findings in more depth. Each focus group was recorded and focus group members' identities were anonymised in the transcripts.

One of the benefits of the focus groups was that we had part-icipation from key agencies that had not been part of the national survey, for example, the police, the Crown Prosecution Service (CPS), Child and Adolescent Mental Health Service (CAMHS), restorative justice managers, a virtual school head and specialist organisations providing diversionary activities. It was also helpful for different professionals to debate the key issues with each other and for us to get a sense of how they worked together.

The quantitative data from the national survey were analysed using a number of statistical analyses with PASW statistical software. The qualitative open response data from the survey and the data from the focus groups were analysed using thematic analysis assisted by NVivo software.

We have brought these data together under the following sub-headings, as these were used to structure both the survey and the focus group discussions, i.e. local authority policy, targets and strategies for reducing offending by looked after children; assessment, planning and review; prevention; care placements; intervention; transition to adulthood; and interagency working.

Although the issues are discussed under these broad headings, some topics feature under a number of headings, for example, the role of restorative justice and practice in interagency working.

Local authority policy, targets and strategies for reducing offending by looked after children

Across the country in diverse local authorities, service managers for looked after children and for youth offending were clearly taking the question of reducing offending by looked after children seriously at a policy and practice level, recognising the specific needs of the group of looked after young people who are involved, as offenders, with the youth justice system. As discussed above, this is generally a small minority of both youth offending and looked after children populations. However, it represents high risk and high need young people, for whom both LAC and youth offending services may be drawn into high cost interventions to prevent escalation of harm by young people to themselves and to others, and for whom, if interventions are not successful, criminal careers may continue into adulthood at great cost to the young people as individuals and to society.

Offending by looked after children was seen both as a separate and shared responsibility. Although LAC service managers were more likely to consider themselves as working towards performance targets (67%) than YOS managers (48%), YOTs were seen as having the primary expertise in this area. This difference in relation to targets is likely to be because of the national outcome data collection for looked after children, which included the C18 statistic for children age 10 to 17 looked after for more than a year and cautioned or sentenced in the previous year compared to that of the local community population. Where local authority targets existed, they were likely to be framed in relation to this comparative rate, because those were the data available; for example, a target might be to reduce the LAC offending rate to the same level as the general population locally or at least to the national average on this indicator. However, some local authorities were setting more specific local targets, e.g. one local authority set a target of reducing offending by 50 per cent in their residential homes.

In the survey and the focus groups, questions were raised about the extent to which the nationally collected outcome data that contributed to these local targets was helpful. It did allow for year on year monitoring but only captured part of the picture, i.e. it did not include those young people looked after for less than a year, did not discriminate between minor and more serious offences, and also did not discriminate between those who had first offended before or after becoming looked after. There were also major difficulties for local authorities in taking account of the placement of their children outside of local authority boundaries *and* their provision of services for children from other local authorities placed in their area – an issue that came up repeatedly for local authorities in both collecting accurate data and in building policy and strategies.

Such difficulties were not only in relation to LAC data, but also in relation to the national standards for the youth offending service. It was suggested that local youth offending teams may appear to do poorly or indeed well because of the work of other YOTs with children placed out of area, while not getting credit for the work they themselves undertook with all children placed in their catchment area. The placement of children across local authority and YOT boundaries therefore raised general difficulties for data management, not only in terms of tracking numbers but also in terms of measuring outcomes.

One of the challenges, therefore, that was raised in relation to policy-making and outcome-based strategic planning was the problem of data collection and management. Most obviously, there were the difficulties of keeping track of children placed out of or into the local authority, but generally there were problems at a more basic level for the YOTs, in terms of collecting and aggregating data specifically for children looked after/in care, and for LAC managers, in collecting and analysing data on offending by children in their care.

In some ways this difficulty is not surprising. From the YOTs' point of view it can be hard to track the offending of children who may move in and out of care, especially if they are accommodated under section 20 – or if they move into or out of secure accommodation/custody. From the LAC management point of view, recording systems are often focused on individual children's files rather than enabling the aggregation of data, such as care plans or offending, at an agency level. There were many concerns in agencies across the country that generally there are insufficient aggregated data, e.g. it was possible to find information on individual files, such as the legal status, type of placement or care plan, but this was not aggregated for all young people in either service to enable YOS and LAC senior managers to identify trends and plan/monitor services.

However, from the focus groups it was possible to see the difference that good data collection and management could make. At best, YOS information managers were able to provide very detailed reports for both LAC and YOS service heads in relation to information on individual children and aggregated across the authority. One YOS information manager commented on how much more efficient this had become since having instant access to LAC databases, enabling him to identify reasons for care, placement histories and the range of agencies involved, etc. as soon as a looked after young person became known to the YOS. He could also track patterns of placement, whether placed in or out of the authority, and follow up with other YOS information managers. More strategically, he could identify the practice of different independent service providers, for example, in terms of moving children, which could be valuable information for commissioners. He could also track occasions when such providers might be placing a group of their more problematic children in one particular home in another area or indeed placing a group of children from another area into his authority, thus potentially moving offending peer groups around. This information manager was able to supply detailed aggregated data on a regular basis regarding age, gender, type of offence and placement patterns in relation to offending to inform strategic managers, policy-makers and practice. As this was one of the largest authorities in the country, senior managers needed detailed information in order to plan services – and this was also a good demonstration of what is possible where the services work closely together and importance is attached to data management.

Whatever the quality of the data available, it was clear from service managers that varied *strategies* for prevention and intervention that were developing had implications in both services for management at all levels and for practitioners. Local authorities described a number of strategies for tackling offending by looked after children, most of which involved aspects of interagency working at different levels in the organisations: for example, regular dyadic LAC and YOS service manager meetings; regular multi-agency meetings to include not only LAC and YOS but also education, CAMHS, the council's legal section; co-location of staff, e.g. LAC social workers seconded to YOT teams; specialist appointments, e.g. social workers/or YOT workers with responsibility for LAC offenders, who could develop protocols and promote constructive approaches that reduced the risk of offending and avoided inappropriately drawing children in care into the criminal justice system.

What emerged was that, although it was regarded as important to have a forum with full participation from a wide range of agencies, including named individuals of sufficient seniority in their own agency, to deliver on commitments, the specific relationship between the two key committed senior managers with responsibility for looked after children and for youth offending was critical at a policy development and implementation level in being able to make a case for prioritising this group of offenders in care, argue for resources, and develop and monitor co-ordinated services.

Assessment, planning and review

Assessment is relevant at each stage of a child's pathway through care and also during contact with the YOS. So the LAC and Asset[3] frameworks that are considered here have particular significance when a child is first in contact with the two systems, but continue to inform planning and reviewing of children's needs and progress. These are agreed national frameworks that set out how the assessment, planning and reviewing should be done in some detail, as in the care planning regulations and guidance (DCSF, 2010a) and the IRO Handbook (DCSF, 2010b), which sets out the role of the Independent Reviewing Officer, including in relation to young people at risk of or offending.

Assessment of any looked after child must focus on the child's development and psychosocial needs, the risks and protective factors in the child, and the people and systems around him or her that will determine the likelihood of those needs being met. One of those needs will be to follow a pro-social/non-offending route into adulthood. The assessment and care planning process for very young children may not have this directly as a focus in the way it will for adolescents, some of whom may already be at risk through, for example, anti-social behaviour or drug-taking. Our survey and focus groups focused on services for looked after young people at immediate risk of offending. But it was almost universal for practitioners from both LAC and YOS teams to comment on the significance of trying to assess and meet children's needs earlier in childhood so that they did not reach this point of risk as adolescents.

The assessment processes by the looked after children and youth offending teams were described by practitioners as having some overlaps in information to be gathered, but also sharing some of the same challenges, especially in relation to properly capturing each child or young person's history:

---

[3] Asset was a structured assessment tool used by YOTs in England and Wales for all young offenders who came into contact with the criminal justice system. (As of 2014/15, Asset is to be updated to AssetPlus.)

They both suffer from the same problem; they don't tell you enough about the genesis of the difficulties. (LAC, focus group)

There were felt to be similarities in LAC and Asset in terms of their holistic approach, but differences regarding risk of offending:

They are from the same school of ecological approaches towards assessment, but there is something about the assessment of risk with regards to offending which is actually qualitatively different. (YOT, focus group)

Although practitioners described them as using an ecological framework that takes account of a range of contextual factors, the LAC and YOT assessments follow quite different structures. The LAC review system, established in the early 1990s, relies on assessment of the seven LAC dimensions to identify the needs of the child or young person. This informs the care plan, which would include placement choice but also the provision of services to promote well-being and reduce risk of harm of all kinds. As practitioners commented, all aspects of the LAC care plan have the potential effect of increasing or reducing risk of offending in the short, medium or long term, e.g. placement choice (including geographical factors); support packages that include mental health services or education; and contact arrangements with birth families. The Asset system, first established by the Youth Justice Board in 2000, was equally well established in the youth offending service, and provided details of the child's characteristics and circumstances, with a focus on the risk of offending but which had come to include a special emphasis on mental health.

Both forms of assessment were deemed to have some specific limitations:

LAC reviews often concentrate on the areas of placement, education, contact and health and often just briefly look at offending behaviour if it is an issue or the young person is a prolific young offender. (Welsh County Council, LAC survey)

There were therefore concerns about how well the LAC review process was able to identify the early signs of risk of offending, e.g. where young people might have money from undisclosed sources or appear to be under pressure that might be from gang violence.

Again, as practitioners commented, there is a balance to be struck between asking a question about offending at LAC reviews on all children, which would give the unfounded and potentially stigmatising message that all children in care are at risk of offending, and not asking questions where there is evidence of risk through challenging behaviour or peer/family contacts that may lead to offending. The IROs, who manage the LAC review process, clearly have a major role to play in maintaining awareness of the issue among the professionals and carers while taking account of the circumstances of each case.

Comments were made on the assessment available when children are at risk or offending, and the lack of a complete narrative that would help to clarify both pathways and a young person's likely response to intervention:

Something we encounter a lot in the assessments or referrals we get is the absence of a rich and coherent narrative. I think the nature of these kids means a large proportion of them have had such fractured histories, they've been here, they've been around, there's no one person in their narrative, no one social worker, there's a turnover. All you've got is a snapshot – if at a particular point you are only looking a year back, and this isn't uncommon, and you don't understand that this child had a diagnosis of autism aged three which somehow got lost, then your interventions are meaningless. That's not an uncommon experience – there is very little connection between the assessment and the likelihood of success in intervention . . . the assessment is itself part of a fragmented approach and when we looked at interventions, for example, in relation to children who have entered the care system, they are extensive. Some children have had several parenting interventions, several counselling and therapeutic interventions, and the assessment is making a recommendation for more. (CAMHS, focus group)

In addition to comments on the Asset and LAC review assessments, there were comments by managers and practitioners on a number of structures and procedures designed to identify risk but also, it was emphasised in one focus group, to identify vulnerability. These may be Cause for Concern Panels, or Risk Panels, or those designed to review and reassess, such as the Case Planning Review Meetings. These were initiated within the YOS but were multi-agency. There may be differences in the timing and criteria for referral to these panels in different agencies, but they seemed to play an important role not only in assessing risk but also in engaging agencies in offering support where need was identified.

More controversial was the weight which was or should be given by risk assessors within the YOS to the fact of a child being looked after. On the one hand, the child in care may be deemed to be safe and cared for, but on the other hand, there will be additional risks in their background and, perhaps, if there is instability or lack of appropriate monitoring in their care placement, from their care status. One local authority had decided, after some disagreements, to classify all looked after children as "medium risk", although this had been successfully challenged by one young person in a stable long-term foster placement and after a first offence, who was angry about assumptions being made simply because she was in care.

One YOT manager talked of the importance of the shift in his service towards paying attention to *vulnerability* as well as *risk* of harm to self or others as part of the risk panel process:

The Youth Offending Service introduced a risk panel process where we look at all young people we've assessed as being high or very high risk of harm to the public and we also look in those panels at their levels of assessed vulnerability. At the start of this I was very clear that the YOTs are the experts at risk of harm and that social care were the experts at vulnerability, and so we only looked at vulnerability if there was a link to risk of harm. But over the years we've shifted on that, because I think we've had to really, because vulnerability is much more a concern for us in our service and our ability to contribute to plans for that has increased, so our staff are much more active in the work that they are doing with the young people. There may be a big focus on welfare which didn't used to be the case and we do hold those risk panels on young people who have high or very high levels of vulnerability, even if the risk of harm to the public is not significant, so I think we've moved on. (YOT, focus group)

One area that attracted discussion was the need for better assessment of mental health needs that were significant for increased risk of offending and were common among looked after children:

I think the one dimension that's missing from both (LAC and Asset) is the assessment of mental health. I think that's a really significant issue. I'm not saying that children who enter care are likely to go on to have full involvement with mental health services . . . but actually a lot of them do have undiagnosed mental health issues and conduct disorders and that's a fairly significant missing component of assessment. (CAMHS, focus group)

It has finally been accepted when a child comes into care for over four months, which is the threshold we use, we do the SDQ. An administrator then feeds it into the database and if the score is over a certain level it triggers an automatic referral to CAMHS, who then triangulate it with the score and the social worker and you get the full SDQ. We are up to 85 per cent compliance with the SDQ including the annual review of the SDQ. (LAC Manager, focus group)

Although there were some concerns about using the SDQ in individual cases for assessment or monitoring progress, it was seen as a helpful starting point. Other local authorities were also using the SDQ as a screening tool to prompt further, more detailed assessment and the significant role of specialist mental health resources for LAC and for YOS in following up such concerns was emphasised.

An important element of assessment for these children involved in several services was the process of presenting the child's history/risk/ vulnerability to the court in the pre-sentence report (PSR). It was agreed that, where a young person was looked after, this process would or certainly should always include input from the child's LAC social worker. The CPS representative in one focus group reported that, if the welfare case for a particular disposal was well argued in the PSR, the courts were likely to go with the recommendation – for all children, but including those looked after:

I don't think the court will look at it and say here's a PSR on a child that's had a really difficult life, that's not looked after, we're going to sentence him one way and here's a PSR on a looked after child that's had a difficult life, so we're going to be more lenient. It's about a true reflection of the difficulties that young person has experienced that's likely to have impacted on their behaviour. In our area we have an incredibly welfare minded court, the majority of the time. (CPS, focus group)

Young people's living arrangements though could be taken into account as a risk factor, according to another CPS focus group member, which may affect how looked after children in residential care or semi-independent hostel accommodation are sentenced:

When you get a group of five regular offenders all living in the same place and one of them comes up for sentence, and the other four have been into court in the last four or five weeks and the magistrates know and the clerk realises and the prosecutors know, whether you send them back in there either on a sentence or anything, you are sending them back in there with other people who have offended recently on similar matters. (CPS, focus group)

Often more variable and difficult to achieve was the presence at court of someone *in loco parentis* for looked after children, not only to support the young person but also to respond to questions regarding their circumstances, the context of the offence and the protective arrangements that could be put in place to prevent re-offending in the event of a non-custodial sentence. The attendance of a social worker or appropriate professional with the young person was seen by all, especially the CPS, as very important in all cases (a point confirmed by members of the Magistrates Association from the research project stakeholders' group). There was a discussion about who needed to attend court and agreement that the most useful was the person who knew the young person best, which may be a foster carer, residential worker or social worker. But it was also important to have someone there able to act on behalf of the corporate parent, the local authority – which may not be the carer.

Prevention

The concept of "prevention" of offending among looked after children and the strategies that might support it were interpreted by diverse professionals as including a range of important organisational and practice issues. As this example below suggests, the lead may come from the YOS:

> *The YOS has now become the strategic lead in improving LAC offending rates. A new plan, simpler, with fewer actions but more impact focused, has been developed – protocols between partners are being updated to incorporate gate-keeping mechanisms to prevent reporting to the police of minor offending where there is no victim other than the corporate parent; the YOS Management Board monitors data on a regular basis; there are actions to ensure that targeted intervention such as Police Community Resolution or referral to the local Youth Inclusion and Support Panel (YISP) are more effectively used and that there is greater joining up with the local tiered approach to managing anti-social behaviour.* (English Metropolitan Council, YOT survey)

A number of these strategies will be further discussed elsewhere in the report, but given this multi-agency, multi-dimensional approach, it seemed helpful to think about prevention in relation to offending by looked after children in three different ways:

- prevention of first offending;;
- prevention of re-offending/escalation of offending
- prevention of criminalisation – looked after children being inappropriately drawn into the criminal justice system.

Prevention of first offending

The prevention of first offending for looked after children needs to be understood in relation to two important areas of activity – those provided within looked after children services and those provided by the youth offending service. For looked after children the goal of care is the well-being of children in all areas of their lives and "prevention of offending" may start at any stage from the care of children in early childhood to the care of 15- or 16-year-olds recently accommodated, who may be vulnerable following abuse and/or may already be at risk of anti-social behaviour and offending. Within the youth offending service, it is more likely that the intervention will be focused on responding to older children who have started to show some conduct problems or anti-social behaviour, signalling a direct risk of offending, although the YOT workers will also be paying attention to areas such as parenting, education and mental health, which affect both offending and more general well-being.

Prevention of first offending – by services for looked after children

Prevention of first offending is clearly not only a concern for the youth offending service, but is also the focus of activities in the LAC services, although often indirectly. In some respects one could argue that the process of removal into care of children at risk of significant harm from infancy to adolescence is one step towards reducing the likelihood of that child subsequently engaging in anti-social or offending behaviour. Therefore, all efforts that are made to promote benefits, such as placement stability, a sense of permanence, mental health and education for looked after children, will be promoting pro-social behaviour and making a significant contribution to reducing the likelihood of offending – important in the context of the known and shared interacting risk factors for care and offending, such as abuse and loss, and also given the potential for promoting resilience in positive placements.

A great deal of the targeted work described in the survey by LAC managers and practitioners across England and Wales that is relevant here is about how children who have a range of emotional and behavioural problems due to their experiences of abuse and neglect can be helped to overcome those difficulties, so that their behaviour does not escalate into mental health problems and/or offending. Although, as discussed earlier, in any one year only a small minority (7% in 2011) of looked after children aged 10 to 17 are cautioned or convicted, it is clear that, as most looked after children have some combination of individual, family, education and community environmental risk factors for offending, attention has to be paid to identifying those who appear to be most at risk and strategies for reducing that risk.

In the survey and focus groups a number of approaches were described, starting with strategic approaches to interagency working and the need for appropriate assessment of emotional and behavioural needs and then treatment – the latter being particularly influential where there were specialist CAMHS for looked after children which could respond to assessed need. There was also a wide range of inter-ventions/preventive activities programmes for looked after children that were designed to enhance their well-being generally, but again were viewed by practitioners as part of the strategy that would reduce the risk of offending for looked after children with different degrees of risk.

The goal of the corporate parent, agreed among practitioners, must be to provide all looked after children with security and resilience, confidence and competence, and a sense of identity and belonging – and for some children this combination will have the specific effect of reducing or even eliminating the risk of offending that might have been expected from their family histories and peer group affiliations. These protective factors can occur in a range of places, including the placement relationships, education, health provision and activities in the community.

Concerns were expressed by a range of professionals that, although it was important not to assume that all children in care were potential or likely offenders, nevertheless behaviour problems that could escalate into offending or emotional problems, and which could lead to a child becoming out of control and aggressive, did mean that there needed to be preventive, therapeutic parenting and other interventions available from the time a child first comes into care. Each placement therefore needs to understand the link between constructive caregiving, pro-social behaviour and reducing offending, as well as picking up at an early stage the signs of offending. This is discussed below in the section on care placements.

Prevention of first offending – by the youth offending service

Early interventions within the youth offending service designed to prevent first offending and involvement with the criminal justice system were most commonly described by agencies in relation to the Youth Inclusion Support Panel (YISP) teams, which sought to prevent social exclusion, offending and anti-social behaviour, by offering support services, primarily to high-risk eight to 13-year-olds, though some teams said they also worked with slightly older children.

The potential service for looked after children from these teams needs to be understood in terms of the more general role of the teams, i.e. for children at risk of offending in the wider community. The survey suggested, and focus groups confirmed, that these teams were positioned in very varied ways in their organisations, but generally with the aim of maintaining links to the youth offending service while operating separately. In some cases the separation is reinforced by the fact that preventive services are commissioned from the voluntary sector. Models ranged from complete separation of the prevention team from the day-to-day running of the YOTs, to the prevention service being very much linked to the YOT, with staff working closely together.

In one of the shire counties with close working relationships at staff/office level, the prevention service was nevertheless said to be carefully badged with a very positive name and took care not, for example, to use YOS premises for work with young people. The model practised in this service was described as "task centred" and used the three-month intervention period as both a time to ensure that the young person understood the seriousness of behaviour that could escalate into offending and a window of opportunity to engage young people in constructive activities that they believed could be life-changing for some of them. A shire council YISP manager described his experience:

When the YISP was launched, the Home Office did a lot of research and one of the most powerful pieces of research was the evidence that when young people were engaged with activities, meeting regularly with their peers, building up self-esteem, they're less likely to offend. It's building up a resilience to offending so we do a lot of work ... I got one lad into the boxing club down the road and within three months his mother was saying he was a different fellow, his eye contact was better, he was going two to three times a week to tournaments and things. The other therapies weren't working, but that changed his life. So for some people it really does do a great deal and for others it's not so powerful. (YISP Manager, focus group)

The emphasis here – and one which was reflected in the survey and other focus groups – is on constructive activity as a key part not only of diversion, but also as more profoundly influencing a child's self-esteem, sense of competence, pro-social values and relationships with family members. Overall, the aim was to build resilience that would enable young people to cope with the risk factors, such as pressure from anti-social peers or family members, which might lead to offending.

There were mixed views expressed both in the survey and the focus groups about the common time limit of three months for prevention work. In this example, there was a very positive approach to an intensive involvement for a fixed period, which focused on enabling the child and their family to find and build on their own strengths and work with them to identify supports in the community. Other professionals argued that some vulnerable children needed longer-term support for themselves and their families:

Extended support and intervention for young person – three months is not always enough time to gain the young person's trust and engagement and meet all needs to prevent re-offending. (English Unitary Council, YOT survey)

So if the YISP involvement was time limited, it was suggested that it was important to ensure that other family support services or perhaps befriending for the young person or indeed a CAMHS intervention was available for the young person and their family to move on to.

How then might this service, which was generally seen as successful for certain children in the community, connect to the goal of preventing offending by looked after children? The question of referral of looked after children to offending prevention teams produced polarised reactions from managers and practitioners in both the survey and the focus groups.

On the one hand, it was suggested that referral to a youth offending prevention team should not be necessary, since looked after children already have a range of support services, and as resources for prevention services are scarce they should be targeted at children with no support:

Where a child is looked after I struggle to see a role for prevention services when that child not only has a social worker but care home staff too, all of whom should be providing a higher level of support than we can. The ever tightening criteria for children to become looked after means that restricted services like ours should focus on families and children who have no support. (English Metropolitan Council, YOT survey)

In complete contrast, it was suggested that referral should be considered for all looked after children,

I believe that as soon as a young person becomes LAC, referrals to outside agencies and YISP should be made and not when they offend. (English Unitary Council, YOT survey)

However, although there was a general concern about the high risk of offending, it was acknowledged by most practitioners that not all children in care were on this pathway and many would find it stigmatising to have the issue automatically raised, as some suggested, at every LAC review.

In addition, there were some concerns, apparently also often expressed by foster carers, that referral to an offending prevention agency would create risk and in itself be stigmatising, so any automatic referral would be seen as another blow to the rights of children in care to be treated like other children in the community. There were also acknowledgements of concerns from foster carers about introducing vulnerable young people to more established offenders:

Some foster carers have concerns about young people engaging in interventions delivered by the YOS Prevention Team, specifically group work, as they are concerned about exposure to more experienced offenders from the youth offending service. (English Metropolitan Council, LAC survey)

There was little mention in the survey or focus groups of the potential role of YOS prevention teams in offering training, advice or consultation to LAC social workers and foster carers. However, a number of authorities had created specialised positions within the YOS for working preventively with looked after children. In some authorities, a social worker was appointed to the prevention team, and in others, a ROLAC (reducing offending by looked after children) worker delivered services to looked after children as well as to children on the edge of care, which did include assisting case managers in understanding the risks and the potential interventions that might be available.

The broad focus on constructive activities as a form of prevention was seen as valuable by most agencies and practitioners concerned with looked after children at risk. In addition to targeted YISP schemes, several local authorities were benefiting from national activity programmes, such as Positive Activities for Young People, and were using these community-based schemes as a non-stigmatising way of helping young people in care and at risk of offending. It was not clear whether data were collected on the use of such initiatives specifically for looked after children or in relation to their risk of offending, but the need to provide activities for children in care as part of or in addition to promoting their education was an area that was widely highlighted as a significant contribution to prevention.

Constructive activity was not the only focus, however, and some prevention services worked on nurturing young people's relationships, based on attachment theory, and planned a longer intervention as a result:

Our Early Intervention Programme works alongside children and young people for a period of approximately six months, using attachment theory very much as the foundation that underpins the content of our sessions of intervention. We meet with young people each and every week at the same time, in the same place (although obviously there is some flexibility in this) and always endeavour to be warm, kind, reliable, consistent, calm, available, trustworthy, honest, genuine, congruent, boundaried, clear, firm and responsive in order to reflect the characteristics of a secure attachment. Being treated in the manner of a secure attachment style is often a new experience for our young people and this can be extremely powerful due to its inherent characteristics and unfamiliarity. We are also mindful about the venues we use to meet young people, as these should be warm, friendly, safe, comfortable and appropriate. (English County Council, YOT survey)

Feeling secure and better able to trust reliable others for help is an important part of developing resilience – and also a way of starting to resolve certain emotional and mental health difficulties. Also valuable is the development of the capacity to think flexibly and empathically and, as has been developed for adult offenders, there are prevention programmes that train young people at risk of offending in flexible thinking skills. Support for speech and language development was also seen as valuable to young people in promoting social skills. Described below is a programme that combines this with creative activities and with helping parents to tune into and offer positive parenting to their children, including those having contact with their children in care. It is likely to be this kind of multi-dimensional package, which tackles the risk from a number of individual and family relationship angles, that will be more successful:

> Our "clever thinking" programme has proven successful over the year looking at all areas of the young person's life. Also we are about to plan a joint initiative with LAC and the local theatre looking at taster sessions for at risk/vulnerable YP doing arts/ drama and music. The Incredible Years Parenting Programme is also something that is offered, even to parents that have had their children removed, to support them with contact time with their child. (English Unitary Council, YOT survey)

Prevention of re-offending or escalation of offending

Although prevention of first offending was clearly important, there was a recognised need to focus on prevention of re-offending or escalation of offending – escalation both of the seriousness of offences and the level of response within the criminal justice system. Many young people may have shown anti-social behaviour or committed minor offences, with some incidents having led to arrest but others simply brought to the attention of family members, caregivers or professionals as a cause for concern, indicating that action needed to be taken.

Many of the strategies described in the previous section were equally valid here as a response to risk of further offending (i.e. diversion, re-education, nurture, working with parents/caregivers) and these are clearly core strategies. However, several developing areas of practice were identified from the survey and focus groups in relation to how first/early minor offences can be dealt with to prevent escalation.

The first strategy is linked to police activity and new types of intervention designed to prevent acceleration of young people into and through the criminal justice system. The most striking change reported was in the use of "neighbourhood" or "community resolutions" – not specific to looked after children, but a change in practice that could also benefit them. Police officers in three of the four focus groups reported now being encouraged to tackle minor offences through a process underpinned by *restorative justice* principles. This was said to be a radical shift from the previous practice of routinely bringing charges. The process – a kind of formalised "street RJ" – required identifying the young person who had committed the offence, recording the young person's details, arranging for the perpetrator to meet with the victim, and the potential to undertake some kind of individual or community reparation. This policy, said by those who mentioned it to have been introduced in autumn 2010, was described by one police officer as 'a return to common sense, good old-fashioned policing'. It was recognised that a key aspect of the development of this policy was that community resolutions were formally recorded as an appropriate and measurable response, i.e. this was seen as legitimate policing activity.

Although it was relatively early days, this policy was said to be having a significant effect in some areas on the number of youth cases coming to court. In one area the number of days that the youth court was sitting had been cut, although this may also have been due to a general reduction in youth crime or other factors. This development of more restorative approaches at street level needs to be monitored. The fact that the child's details are recorded and therefore known to the police can mean that the offence is brought to the attention of other agencies, which may be helpful, but it may also be taken into account if there is a subsequent offence. So this approach is not equivalent to a less formal and non-recorded use of restorative justice as a way of handling a minor incident, for example, by a worker or even police officer in a residential home.

The link between restorative justice and a community-based

approach was also a feature of another intervention that was described in one London Borough. Here other prevention services were under threat from cuts, but they had developed a screening system of "triage" by the YOS, which engaged at an early stage with young people committing more minor offences in a similar restorative process to the community resolution by the police. This system may be able to identify at an early stage young people, especially those in care, who need help and support to avoid further risk of offending.

Again, within children's services there were strategies that were designed to enhance the well-being of looked after children, but which also provided diversionary and educational/employment-focused experiences that could reduce the risk of offending:

Social services have set up a work experience scheme which ran over the summer holidays. Even though it was not specifically targeting young offenders, some of those LAC who attended were also involved with the YOS for offending behaviour. This resulted in time being occupied during the long summer holiday and the young people received a new experience and offending behaviour reduced for this time period. (Welsh County Council, LAC survey)

Prevention of looked after children being inappropriately drawn into the criminal justice system

The need to prevent the criminalisation of looked after children through being inappropriately drawn into the criminal justice system has long been recognised as one of the major challenges for those involved with older looked after children. Where children's challenging behaviour, often but not only in residential care, results in criminal charges being brought, then this adds lifelong risk to the already high-risk lives of children from backgrounds of abuse and neglect who are in the care of the state.

There will be situations where troubled children from problematic family backgrounds will commit such serious offences, which threaten the safety of other children and adults, that involvement of the criminal justice system will be necessary and appropriate. But there are many cases where challenging or anti-social behaviour, such as damage to the fabric of a residential care building, which may be directly linked to young people's histories of abuse (e.g. mental health problems, learning and emotional difficulties) or indeed their care status and situation (e.g. being placed at a distance from family members, being moved between placements), is then not handled constructively at an interpersonal level in the placement and/or leads directly to police involvement and prosecution. In spite of long-standing recommendations/requirements for protocols between children's services and the police – and especially between residential home staff and the police – there remain concerns regarding the extent to which charges are still brought for minor offences. As a result, looked after children may be drawn into the youth justice system inappropriately and in ways that can lead to an escalation of emotional and behavioural problems, while also reducing the likelihood of young people getting back into education, training and employment.

Alongside these concerns it was accepted in the survey and focus group responses that *restorative justice* is well established in most areas and was a positive benefit – but also that it was diverse in its applications:

We have used restorative approaches with a number of young people placed in residential care settings. This has been successful in avoiding criminal justice action, especially with violent incidents between young people and their carers. (Residential Manager, London Borough, survey)

Restorative justice is suggested as an alternative to arrest and charging when young people commit offences, not only in residential care but also in foster care:

Some individual foster carers understand the restorative agenda very well and are very proactive to ensure that young people are not criminalised. This needs capturing and embedding in induction and training as part of the RJ strategy – some work to do. (English County Council, LAC survey)

The three main agencies involved – youth offending, LAC services and the police – all reported playing a role in implementing restorative justice, from "street RJ" through managing behaviour in residential care to more formal victim/offender conferences, for offences from the more minor to the most serious, including within the young offenders institutions.

Where areas are more successful in developing this work, there are generally restorative justice managers or specialist workers who take a lead in implementing but also training staff in restorative justice:

Having a dedicated restorative justice officer who could deliver training to workers has been very beneficial as it has empowered workers. (English County Council, LAC survey)

These organisational commitments to restorative justice, especially training, were emphasised as essential because, for example, of the staff turnover that affected the residential care sector. Courts were also said to be supportive of restorative approaches and this could be reflected in sentencing.

The views of all disciplines was that restorative justice was a power-ful tool, especially in residential care, where practice had changed most significantly in these local authorities, as this residential manager described, contrasting previous and current practice:

If a child had a temper tantrum and threw some cups across the kitchen, they would call the police and that child would be done for criminal damage. That achieves nothing except criminalising that child. We now have sanctions, active sanctions. We will sit that child down and say, why did you do that, we've got to go over to Tescos now, we don't have a budget to replace these cups so how are you going to help us out with that? They will pay out of their own money the cost of replacing them. They will go over to the shops with a member of staff, choose new mugs. It may sound like a small thing but they have had a role in that, they have investment. They tend not to get broken again. We had a child who recently destroyed our BBQ area, he's agreed to rebuild it. He's not going to break it again if he built it. (Residential Manager, focus group)

Or in offender/victim conferences:

It's difficult to judge how effective restorative justice is when a young person has got that as part of their plan. But I can tell you from experience, anecdotal evidence, young people have met with their victims, and I think victim take-up on these programmes is often quite low, the young people that have been confronted with their victims – it is very, very powerful. Young people talk, young people cry when they are faced by what they have done. They end up in tears. (YOT, focus group)

Restorative justice was linked to another important strand of work with young offenders, *victim empathy*. Discussion around restorative justice and victim empathy highlighted the fact that young people in care were sometimes seen as less able to participate in aspects of restorative justice because of their lack of empathy and remorse. They were, in particular, more likely to be screened out of conferences because they seemed unable to move towards a position of accepting the impact of their behaviour on other people. It was recognised that this was due to young people's history of abuse and neglect that had damaged their capacity to reflect on their feelings and those of other people:

We are aware that, given the emotional damage that many looked after children have accrued, it would not be a productive meeting for either of them. So we probably screen out more young looked after people from that face to face than we would an average cohort of offenders. (YOT, focus group)

Young people in care need additional help if they are not going to be ruled out of the restorative justice conference process. Where restorative justice was being used in residential homes, it was perhaps possible to build some of this "emotional intelligence" in young people

– but clearly the implication is that, where possible, looked after young people generally need more help earlier and when younger in foster or residential care in developing the capacity for social cognition/ emotional intelligence and empathy.

The emphasis on restorative "approaches" or "practices" as well as conferences emerged from the experiences of a wide range of practitioners. There was some concern about the resources needed for each conference:

> *I don't want to say this but the amount of resources that go into one conference are massive and you can put weeks' worth of work in and then somebody doesn't turn up and it doesn't go ahead and we can't work like that, we don't have those resources. I think there's some quite innovative work going on in terms of working with victims and mediation, using video, audio recordings to translate messages from victims to offenders, so it's extremely good. But the actual conferencing, I don't think we can.* (YOT, focus group)

One further factor in thinking about the practice of restorative justice was the alternative or complementary use of the concept and practice of *mediation*. In one shire county focus group, it was suggested that restorative justice was a less sophisticated form of mediation, though both were still used.

There was a range of multi-agency approaches that agencies were using to tackle the risk of criminalisation to looked after children at a strategic and practice level employing restorative justice approaches, including police officers working with young people in residential care homes. This included, as one residential manager explained, having a seconded officer who was involved not only in speaking to young people about how to manage their lives and friendships to reduce the risk of offending, but also in sporting and social activities. Here, too, restorative approaches were built into the way in which young people's behaviour was managed and into the role of the police officer. Although most agencies had protocols for managing offences within the residential home restoratively and avoiding taking cases to court, it seemed that these arrangements were likely to be more successful where there were good working relationships with specific police officers, who also got to know the young people and had the trust of the group.

Key here are all the stages in the process that lead to a young person in care being brought before the court, each potentially providing an opportunity for diversion. In the first place, there are all the stages, discussed above by managers and practitioners, that should be leading to a situation where looked after children receive good quality care and the kind of support that enables them to manage their strong feelings and behaviour and to adopt pro-social values so that they do not get drawn into behaviour that can be defined as criminal. But where challenging or anti-social behaviour occurs, there are various stages (mostly subject to local or national protocols), from the judgements made by residential care staff and the police to those of the CPS, at which checks and balances need to be available to ensure that looked after children are not disadvantaged by their status and placement circumstances.

Care placements – reducing risk and promoting resilience

Here, as elsewhere in the study, when thinking about risk and resilience in relation to different placements, we had to take into account the nature of placements that contributed to *good welfare outcomes*, such as educational success, resilience and stability, alongside and linked to preventing *offending outcomes* and contact with the youth justice system. In the survey and focus groups we invited information and views about a range of placements from foster care through to residential care, supported lodgings, independent living and the secure estate (i.e. young offenders institutions (YOIs), secure training centres and secure children's homes). In the interview and case file study, discussed below, we looked at this across cases.

For most agencies, there were some difficulties regarding beneficial placement choice that cut across placement types. One of the major dilemmas is the *geographical location* – can the young person be placed within the local authority area? There is now a "sufficiency" requirement that the local authority will do whatever is "reasonably practicable" to provide accommodation within its own area (DCSF, 2010c). In London Boroughs, however, concerns were expressed first about the impossibility of placing all children within the borough (the majority of looked after children in some boroughs are placed outside the area), and also the fact that influence from offending peers and gangs was so great in some urban areas that for some young people the only way to reduce risk and promote a more constructive engagement with a placement and with school was to be placed at a distance, even if there were risks of young people running back to the home area and the placement breaking down.

Stability generally was seen as a major challenge, both for some of those young people who had been in care from their earlier years and those who entered care in middle childhood or adolescence. The lack of basic building blocks, such as regular school attendance and nurturing, and pro-social relationships in the family of origin were seen as linked to increased risk of later offending and aggressive behaviour. Where stable placements and high quality care had been achieved, these risks reduced significantly. But if it had not been possible to create stability, the risks were increased, as described by this LAC manager:

I have young people in care who have all exhibited trying to assert control and quite aggressive behaviours and some bullying behaviour and it seems to me that comes from a lack of stability. They are leading quite a rudderless existence, different placements and movement through different placements and care homes, foster homes, whatever it may be. They just don't have that control over their lives, so they seek control over other areas of their life and that does result in very aggressive behaviours. (LAC Manager, focus group)

There were also some specific concerns about placement decisions for the cohort of children *coming into care late*, in their early to mid-teenage years. This may be following maltreatment concerns or family breakdown, which could result from out of control behaviour, possibly including offending. This route often meant accommodation under section 20 (Children Act 1989), where parental responsibility in law remained with birth parents. There were often pleas from practitioners for support to maintain young people more effectively at home in order to avoid coming into care:

> There is an abundance of kids in their teens coming into care relatively late under a section 20 . . . I think that's one of the areas we could look at, reducing the numbers of kids in care. There's got to be more effective ways. (LAC, focus group)

> You do sometimes get children who become looked after through their offending behaviour within the home, where it's got to a position where it gets problematic, in that it's assaults against parents or damaged property, where the parent won't have them in the home anymore. That comes back to being in care for a short period of time and prioritising those young people coming back out of care so we can sustain them better at home with support services. They have entered care for the wrong reasons and they need to go back out. (Residential Manager, focus group)

It is apparent that, although there has been much emphasis on the risk of criminalisation of looked after children, on the basis that behaviour which at home would not lead to police involvement does so in residential care, there are situations where challenging or offending behaviour, which might be managed or tolerated in some families, in other families leads to children being rejected and coming into care, sometimes following arrest and conviction for offences. Although some children who come into care in this way may benefit from reunification with support, there will be some, as there were in this study, for whom care offers a way out of dysfunctional, neglectful or abusive families in adolescence and for whom it should be seen as a positive option.

Foster care placements

For most managers and practitioners, the consensus was that on balance foster care was likely to be protective, and that young people who could be supported in stable foster care would be at less risk of offending. Foster care, and stable family settings more generally, were believed to provide the young person with positive role models, guidance and boundaries, supervision, stability of carer, and to increase the likelihood of access to education, employment and training. These comments were made by LAC social workers in focus groups:

I think the context of fostering is different to start with, in that the child is part of a family unit, not having to compete with lots of other young people, different staff changes on shifts. I think from the outset it's different.

Foster care minimises risk. I don't think there is a linear relationship, but certainly in terms of building attachments, having a positive adult available and engaging the child. They don't have to change education/schools as much. I think that has a positive outcome, certainly on the cases I work with.

A stable and long-term foster placement will usually result in the young person being engaged in education/training. There will be appropriate role modelling by family members and a work ethic.

This emphasis on the role of the foster family and attachment relationships, combined with promotion of life chances through education, was, however, accompanied by concerns that foster carers needed more training/expertise than many had in order to sustain those relationships and provide guidance in the face of troubled, risky and even dangerous behaviours. This was especially difficult when foster homes were caring for children of different ages:

We have found that our in-house foster carers simply cannot manage that level of intensity. If they have two other children in placement who are younger, maybe there will be an influence on the younger ones, and if the youngster's out late or bringing people home or there is [stolen] money under the bed . . . there is a small proportion coming in that are doing some pretty serious stuff. (LAC, focus group)

There are also issues for training foster carers (e.g. in restorative justice approaches) when they are such a large and diverse group:

One of the risks, and it's not just around offending, it's almost how you can get a handle as easily on practice across a very large foster care body as opposed to what is a very narrow residential body. So I think there are issues around the consistency of our foster carers in terms of their response to behaviours. We have done a lot of work with residential workers on what constitutes offending and alternatives to escalation. There are circumstances where foster carers are less responsive to that and you can get foster carers who are behaving in ways that you would prefer they didn't, in terms of ringing the police up for this, that or the other. (LAC, focus group)

Solutions suggested for finding carers who could provide skilled and stable care were both to improve in-house recruitment and to include, in the commissioning process with the independent sector, an expectation that foster carers would need to be able to manage not only the day-to-day care of challenging young people, but also explicitly the support for young people at risk of or with a history of offending. This would include attending court with young people, as discussed above, and working with the YOS.

The development of Multi-dimensional Treatment Foster Care (MTFC) was mentioned by some respondents to the questionnaire. This is a highly specialised and resource-intensive approach to foster care based on social learning theory and developed in the Oregon Social Learning Center, primarily for young people who have anti-social behaviour problems. MTFC is now more widely available in the UK, having been piloted and evaluated here (Biehal *et al*, 2012) and is the focus of a new development initiative from the Department for

Education both for adolescents (MTFC-A) and younger children, (MTFC-C). Although it is a treatment model, and therefore time limited, for some young people staying on in their treatment foster care placement may be possible as a permanence option, in spite of the cost, if a high-risk young person had significantly improved their behaviour and also become part of the family.

Although some local authorities reported taking steps to develop these specialist options, which might reduce risk for adolescents within foster care, others commented that some local authorities had cut schemes for specialist adolescent foster carers and remand foster carers in recent years and they felt less well rather than better resourced for this group of young people:

A lack of robust foster placements for very challenging/criminal justice type behaviours leads to more of our young people than helpful needing residential settings. Overall, the numbers are small, but for each child lost in this type of care, it is a real shame that there are not more foster carers willing to work with this profile. The national shortage of carers allows them to "cherry pick" their children. Specialist projects will take emotionally complex children, but it is the acting out young people with offending behaviour where there is a real gap in the market. (English County Council, YOT survey)

The limited availability of dedicated and specialist carers raised concerns that, although stable foster care could be protective, unstable foster care could increase the risk of offending or re-offending – and was the context for many young people moving to residential care.

Residential care placements

As discussed above, although only a relatively small proportion (around 9%) of looked after young people are in residential care (DfE, 2011a), placement in residential care most commonly follows behaviour problems either in foster care or in the family environment. Children's homes are therefore providing placements for a very particular and often high-risk group of young people (Berridge *et al*,

2011b). In our sample of looked after young people who offended, almost all were in residential care or in semi-independent living following residential care, at the time of interview. The potential links between offending and residential care pathways were described in various ways:

It is, by and large, the case that it is those young people who are at most risk of offending who are placed in residential care, as other forms of care have not been seen to meet their needs. (London Borough, LAC survey)

The young people who find themselves in residential placements may have been through several foster care placements due to behaviours they have exhibited and therefore may be further down the offending route in terms of their behaviours. (English Unitary Council, LAC survey)

The concerns reflected among practitioners and managers in our study were often about how residential care settings could manage the young people's difficult behaviours, including experience of offending or being at risk of offending, while also supporting their vulnerability in terms of mental health and educational needs, given that what the young people also have in common is backgrounds of abuse, neglect and loss. For residential staff, there can be a sense that the latter are at the end of the line, and concern that young people were also affected by this feeling of residential care as a last resort:

To be brutally honest, a residential home is a last resort for looked after children and they are children that, for some reason, are not able to be fostered, and they know that. They come to us from very traumatic backgrounds, having had some awful life experiences, feeling like the child that nobody wants and their self-esteem is through the floor. It's almost inevitable that they're going to get into offending and our job is to prevent that. (Residential Manager, focus group)

However, there were many positive voices regarding residential care and the potential for creating a therapeutic environment to mitigate the impact of previous harm and be protective in relation to offending, with a special focus on building relationships with staff and other young people, as described by this residential care manager:

We work hard to repair the harm these children have already experienced by introducing protective factors into their lives. We will develop the relationship between staff and children, allowing them to observe positive role models and begin to trust in adults. When children are newly accommodated, they will be allocated a child who has been established in the home for a longer period of time to act as their mentor. This helps to encourage positive peer relationships and an opportunity to improve self-esteem through involvement and engagement.

Parents are involved where appropriate in all aspects of the child's care and are encouraged to work with us to reinforce boundaries and encourage social activities and education. Above all else, the home provides a safe and stable environment for the child with continual support and encouragement, rewarding the positives and positively engaging in ways to counteract the negatives. (Residential Manager, English County Council, survey)

A residential home, therefore, was seen by many residential managers as potentially greatly beneficial to vulnerable looked after children who were also offenders, provided that they were given round-the-clock care and thorough risk assessments prior to entering the residential home, which allowed staff to begin working effectively with them from the start.

There was a feeling that residential care could offer more than foster care for especially vulnerable children who needed clear boundaries:

Residential care offers a 24/7 monitoring and engagement pro-vision that can, in most cases, quickly identify offending behav-

iours and consider a multiple of alternative strategies in order to work with young people to reduce and desist from offending behaviours. (English County Council, LAC survey)

Accurate and completed risk assessments prior to admission enable staff to develop strategies to support young people and minimise risks posed. (English Metropolitan Council, LAC survey)

Residential manager respondents also aimed to reduce the risk of offending by supporting the young people to manage relationships with professionals and attend meetings:

To support the young person to maintain the relationship with his/her YOT worker and to keep appointments. Few young people will choose to keep appointments with authority figures if they are not properly supported and encouraged to do so. (Residential Manager, English County Council, survey)

Relationship building between high quality staff and young people was repeatedly cited as the key component to successful residential living. According to some residential managers, "corporate parenting" through relationship-based work provided the structure and support that young people might have lacked in their home lives and/or communities:

Protective factors tend to be around the staff team, their experience and the relationships they build with the children. (English Metropolitan Council, LAC survey)

One residential care manager described her children's home as a model of residential care that was proving to be very successful in providing good care and preventing offending. This was primarily attributed to it being a small, family-like home for four to five young people, having stable and appropriately trained and paid staff, taking an active approach to getting young people into school and activities, and making a commitment to restorative approaches with the active presence of a police officer, who was able to speak with individual young people and work alongside staff with the young people as a group. These factors together were felt by this residential manager to be contributing to a change for the good among the young people:

I think the fact that we are now longer term and we are able to develop relationships and re-create more of a family home atmosphere, where the children feel they have some sense of belonging and some investment because it's their home, certainly we are seeing much less criminal damage, much less. If we go back two or three years, staff cars used to be damaged regularly, staff would be assaulted, windows would be put out on a regular basis. That does not happen anymore. I've never known a staff car to be damaged in the two-and-a-half years I have been there. I believe that's in large part due to the fact that the children have more stability. (Residential Manager, focus group)

These factors were all also valued elsewhere, especially where positive relationships with the police had been developed, as another residential care manager described:

Our relationship with our Safer Neighbourhood Police Team has been an innovation of which we are proud. Initially, when the officers started to attend the home, there were often negative comments about the officers from our residents. However, a regular football game between the team and our residents has improved the relationships and now, three years on, the police are warmly greeted by the young people who also feel safe enough to speak to the officers about many areas of their lives that they would never have told police officers about previously. (Residential Manager, London Borough, survey)

There were critical comments made in areas where protocols and working relationships with the police were not so fully accepted, but also where residential homes were still too big and staff training (including on restorative justice) was hard to achieve in the context of lack of resources and staff turnover.

Restorative justice was described nationally as the dominant approach in residential care in relation to managing difficult behaviour, promoting pro-social behaviour, and avoiding criminalisation. Restorative justice in a residential context is often less about formal perpetrator–victim meetings and more about enabling a young person to reflect on and face up to the consequences of their behaviour, as well as offering some pathway for reparation. "RJ" was described as providing a very constructive way of preventing escalation or repetition of challenging behaviour, but also as being of assistance in preventing the use of more formal routes that lead to arrest and involvement with the criminal justice system.

There was a widespread recognition of the emotional and cognitive difficulties of young people in residential care, who had histories of abuse and neglect and who may struggle to engage in interventions based on restorative justice principles that require a capacity to reflect on their own feelings and behaviour and to understand/have empathy for the minds of others:

Many children in residential care who have experienced early years and ongoing trauma and display complex emotional and behavioural difficulties are not able to make use of RJ in the form that it is implemented in our authority. I strongly believe that this is the case, particularly where children are unable to make appropriate connection with adults in the first place. I have experience of working with children who have attachment disorders of varying levels, all of whom would have displayed offending behaviours and will have a clear inability to engage in an RJ process. (English Metropolitan Council, LAC survey)

One problem with this perspective is that, although it usefully acknowledged a very real difficulty in young people's thinking processes, it may appear to suggest that the impact of early trauma and attachment problems can neither not be challenged or changed by promoting sensitive caregiving in the residential setting, nor that this might be a good reason for persisting with restorative approaches as part of young people's emotional and social education.

Finally, the relationship between the community and the residential home was sometimes seen as having an effect on the young people. The way the community viewed and treated young people in residential homes could have an impact on the young person's success within them. Simultaneously, it was felt that the behaviour of young people within residential homes affected neighbours and from there, the community as a whole. As a result, some residential homes worked hard with the community to establish better relationships and greater understanding:

In my experience the community stigma is an issue with children in residential care. Many people within the community will see children in care as "naughty" children or young offenders and will expect the worst from them. We work within the local community to high profile who we are and what it is we are trying to achieve and in getting the community involved. We have managed to quash some of these stigmas and show local residents that they are just children in need of care and love who have had an unfortunate start in life. (English County Council, LAC survey)

Residential care staff who were untrained did not understand the pathways leading to offending, and did not create effective care plans. Where there was an inadequate number of available staff, this increased risks of offending for looked after children.

A specific issue that emerged for many respondents working with looked after children in residential homes was staff safety. While many residential workers welcomed policies to avoid criminalisation of looked after children within the home, including restorative justice, others were concerned that matters had gone too far, and staff would be unable to protect themselves because of these same policies:

Residential workers do take lots of abuse from young people and they get on with their job. However, it gets to a limit where the worker feels enough is enough and that the police should be called. They feel this right has been taken away from them by managers who have no idea what they go through; they feel it is more to do with statistics than anything else. Restorative justice is a good tool with certain individual young people but it does not work with all and workers feel that their rights are less than the young people's rights. (English Metropolitan Council, LAC survey)

With regards to assaults on residential staff, there seems to be a culture in YOT that 'it comes with the territory' so staff ought not to press charges when they are the victims of assault. Many staff do not press charges but at the same time believe we should be able to come to work without being subjected to physical harm. (Residential Manager, English Unitary Council, survey)

There were also concerns that the tolerant, protected environment of the homes may promote further offending and did not prepare young people for the outside world:

There are also some residential units where the policy is not to criminalise young people for their actions. This has resulted in offences being tolerated rather than reported to the police and dealt with as they would have been in a different placement. This lack of consequences would, in my opinion, lead to further crimes being committed. (Residential Manager, English Unitary Council, survey)

As a unit for young people going into the leaving care programme I often get told that we protect the young people in our care too much because when they go into leaving care they have a false expectation about what they can receive. I believe we are doing the same with the criminality protocol. A young person in our care often used to threaten us physically when we looked after him – he went into independence and was beaten up three times

in a fortnight because he thought he could do the same outside.
(Residential Manager, English Metropolitan Council, survey)

One factor raised in the research review above (Barter, 2007; Berridge *et al*, 2011b) and reflected nationally in this survey was concern about how to manage the *peer relationships* in residential care, which could often make children feel insecure and unsafe as well as lead them into anti-social behaviour and offending. Risks for young people within the home included being encouraged to offend to gain "respect" or encountering bullies who used more vulnerable young people within the home to commit offences on their behalf. Respondents mentioned that it was often easy for criminal activity to be normalised or even for there to develop a pro-offending culture within a home, especially when young people were placed with more experienced offenders. As Berridge *et al* (2011b) have pointed out, children in residential care are in an open environment from which they can go to see friends as well as family members. So young people may be either supported or at risk from young people inside and outside of the home.

A concern about the timing of leaving residential care was raised in one authority where the residential homes were perceived very positively, but the expectation of the local authority was that all children would be moved out of residential care by the age of 17. The paradox this created for the manager of one home was that they accepted 13- to 15-year-olds who were highly vulnerable, with multiple emotional and behavioural problems, sometimes multiple previous placements, often immature and with few social skills and little education. They then worked very effectively with them, got them into school, etc., but from around the time of their 16th birthday, as the plan for them to move on began to be discussed and implemented, the young people started to deteriorate and often offend. Some needy young people were simply not ready for the threat to their security when they were still trying to catch up from their previous losses:

We have a young man who is six months off his 16th birthday, who can't get into his room because it's full of teddies and fluffy toys. (Residential Manager, focus group)

The government initiative, the Right2BCared4 project (2011), promoted the principle that young people aged 16 to 18 should have a greater say in the decision-making process preceding their exit from care (residential and foster care) and that they should not be expected to leave care until they reach the age of 18, but it is unclear how widely these principles have been adopted (Munro *et al*, 2011).

In the current policy climate, children in stable foster care, who are generally less vulnerable, will have the option of staying till 21. It is striking therefore – and certainly not unique to any one authority – that this more vulnerable group are moved to "semi-independence" from residential care just at the critical point in adolescence when continuity of relationships, care and education/training might give them the time and opportunity to establish some resilience, and to have some chance of a stable and pro-social adult life. Residential staff commented that, although they welcomed former residents back and tried to support them after leaving the home, there were few structures to support this and few resources.

The cost and availability of residential care are clearly factors in moving young people on before they are ready, but such policy and practices are high risk and create further problems at the next stage. A leaving care manager commented that young people from residential care need far more support and this then had to be built into a much more fluid living situation where it is harder to help:

This is a very big concern of ours, because all of the young people we have had from residential care couldn't manage semi-independent care. I mean we have a limited number, but the ones we transfer . . . one that is now in a specialist environment . . . and I would say it's more expensive than the residential home he went from. (Leaving Care Manager, focus group)

Not all young people feel vulnerable in semi-independent living, as discussed below, but where there is a policy of moving young people on from residential care at 17, regardless of their capacity to cope, this does appear to be in breach of good practice guidance as well as a) undermining the good work done by staff and b) raising the anxiety and problem behaviour of the other children in the home as they observe others leaving and anticipate their own departure.

In residential care, as in foster care, there were differences in the degree to which local authorities were trying to meet specific young people's needs within their in-house provision or from the *independent residential sector*. The argument given by one London Borough LAC manager for commissioning individual places from private providers rather than developing their own provision was that it allowed local authorities to find very specific placements for very specific needs, e.g. a highly disturbed 10-year-old in need of a therapeutic resource or an older offender with drug use problems would need a different resource. However, there were additional tasks for the local authority and the YOS in relation to risks of offending in making sure that private providers signed up to the expected protocols and practices expected for in-house residential care:

In private sector residential care homes you've got to get in and work with the senior management team and get them to embed this philosophy of reducing offending rates for looked after children into their policies. (LAC, focus group)

It was suggested that, although many private homes were co-operative with this government expectation, Ofsted should enforce a requirement that private sector children's homes show commitment to reducing unnecessary criminalisation through protocols and practices such as restorative justice. Additionally, where young people appeared in court, they were often not well supported when in independent residential homes at a distance from the home authority.

It was clearly a major concern that young people, especially those placed out of area and in independent children's homes, were too frequently not accompanied at court by a representative of the corporate parent, i.e. a social worker from the home local authority. This disadvantaged the young person who may be both unsupported and also not in a position to have his family context and history put to the court in any kind of mitigation.

Where a service was commissioned from a particular provider, there could be groups of young people placed together in a home and community, often away from their home area but with offenders known to them:

You see a lot of young people offending together in our local authority, who know each other through the care system presumably, being put into the same homes elsewhere – and other groups placed in our local authority. (YOT, focus group)

This point was raised by an information manager who was tracking children and placements and who suggested that there does need to be good information and co-ordination to avoid exacerbating rather than solving problems of offending through commissioning from the independent sector.

Finally, one point that is often made regarding residential care, and this study was no exception, is the considerable concern regarding the quality of training of residential workers, and the link between training and the quality of care. The training offered to staff in residential homes was described in the survey as diverse, ranging from behaviour management training to "de-escalation skills", managing substance misuse and mental health. The introduction of social pedagogy in a number of areas had generated interest in the notion of aspiring to a more highly trained workforce with good outcomes:

We have also adopted a social pedagogy model of working which incorporates encouraging the children to take pride in them-selves, their surroundings and their lives. The children have embraced this style of working and have adapted to the head, heart and hand idea by getting involved with projects around the home, taking pride in their work, having their successes made known and celebrated, and admitting the need for help and accepting help from others. (Residential Manager, focus group)

But the initiatives to develop social pedagogy in the UK also high-lighted the absence of an agreed national training scheme or minimum qualification level for residential workers compared to other countries in Europe, where, for example, social pedagogy is at degree level.

Remands into care

Opinions differed as to whether remand into care was on the increase in their areas or not, but one residential manager said that at one point the majority of young people in his establishment had been remanded into care. From the point of view of the residential managers this meant that more challenging young people were arriving in residential homes, with courts having perhaps unrealistic expectations of what could be achieved. However, one representative from the CPS spoke of how courts sometimes used remands into care when they became frustrated that very vulnerable and needy young people were not being removed from damaging families and offered help:

> The courts feel that they are left with a situation where the problem exists, no one in their view has taken a hold of the situation pre-criminalisation of the young person, and the only way of proactively involving the local authority is to remand into the care of the local authority to give them a statutory duty to do something. (CPS, focus group)

It was suggested in one group that there were fewer secure children's homes and this had led to remand to local authority children's homes becoming more common.

The secure estate

The difficulties in working with looked after children in the secure estate were commented on by LAC and YOS workers, both in relation to maintaining contact and managing discharge back to the community.

A key concern for LAC teams working with looked after young people placed in the secure estate was the distance between the placement and the young person's local area. It was difficult for teams to maintain contact with young people in the secure estate due to the economic and time cost to local authorities of travelling to visit them. The distance between the secure estate and the young person's local area also disrupted the young person's contact with family and friends, and interfered with service provision:

> *In the secure estates it can often be difficult for other professionals to gain access to the young people, making it difficult to carry out statutory duties such as reviews and statutory visits. Times to visit are often very restricted and often with little joint working. Visits to the secure estate can often mean long journeys for a very short time with the young person and on occasions can be cancelled at very short notice. There need to be more practical ways of conducting statutory duties that are the same across all secure estates with good information sharing, especially if a young person is moved – it is often days later that social workers find out about a move.* (Welsh County Council, LAC survey)

Some survey respondents identified the difference between the approach of the secure estate and the LAC teams to the young person as a significant practice issue. They saw the approach of the secure estate as punitive rather than care oriented, and expressed concern about the ability of secure units to meet the needs of the young people. Concern was specifically expressed about the lack of understanding in the secure estate about the vulnerabilities of looked after children:

> *Secure units go against the welfare ethos by bringing in a punishment dimension – it is hard in reviews to meet all the criteria about children's needs because of this.* (English County Council, LAC survey)

> *We also come to this as care professionals while the criminal justice system is more intent on people learning from their experiences and being punished (where appropriate).* (English Unitary Council, LAC survey)

Safeguarding issues – to what extent do secure estate staff understand these issues and exercise their responsibilities to safeguard children? (English County Council, LAC survey)

The secure estate rarely offers the type of specialist intervention that effectively addresses the fundamental issues which are likely to increase the chances of reoffending. This is specifically the case in relation to specialist CAMHS/therapy to assist the young person to address causes of emotional problems that often lead to criminal behaviour. (London Borough, LAC survey)

One local authority had been funding a specialist social worker to work with their own children in a local YOI, but the worker also tried to encourage other authorities to be more supportive of their looked after children in custody.

Survey respondents highlighted how difficulties had arisen following the discharge of young people from the secure estate because of the lack of information sharing and communication from the secure estate. One local authority called for clearer guidelines for young people under section 20:

There is a sense that our role is eroded and that the secure unit and the youth offending service arrange meetings, etc. New guidance about our role in such circumstances will help. (English Unitary Council, LAC survey)

Planning for discharge can be difficult and often left to the LA to set up a plan in isolation and without comprehensive knowledge or input from the institution. (London Borough, LAC survey)

Respondents highlighted some of the difficulties that young people who have been in secure accommodation face when they are released, such as adjusting to freedom, finding accommodation, and reintegration:

Consideration has to be given to young people adjusting to an unrestricted environment following a period of detention. (Welsh County Borough Council, LAC survey)

Resettlement can pose additional challenges, with impacts upon families, re-integration at school, picking up with friend-ships/community activities, difficulties securing accommo-dation, etc. (English County Council, LAC survey)

Given the concerns regarding reoffending and longer-term criminal pathways in adulthood, the resettlement of all young people from secure accommodation and custody must be of great concern. For looked after young people who often lack pro-social or indeed any family or peer support at this stage, the risks are considerable.

Supported lodgings/semi-independent living arrangements

The role of living arrangements with some degree of support post-16 was highlighted as very significant. Experiences were very varied in the young people's interviews – discussed below – and this was also reflected in the survey and focus groups. In this area of provision, commissioned providers from the private sector played an important role – and this was seen by local authority commissioners as a way of ensuring diverse provision to match diverse individual need:

The first major thing we did last summer was to commission semi-independent provision – we came up with seven different levels of support. Some young people need support 24/7 and someone sleeping in there, and some have a studio flat with someone on site, right through to you have your own flat and four hours a week of your key worker. And even then some are saying I don't need that, I'm OK, I'm going to college, I have my life reasonably together and I am ready to move into my council flat at 18 . . . and we commissioned that from a small number of providers . . . You might find some young people that have really kicked against fostering, kicked against residential, who do find it liberating or they carry on in the same vein and get into difficulty. It could be offending, really struggling, and it's very difficult for the social worker, personal advisor and key worker to then say, what do we do now? (LAC, focus group)

The need for careful assessment of young people's needs was mentioned in terms of the level of support, but the significance of reliable relationships with key workers, personal advisers and supported lodgings carers was also emphasised. In supported lodgings, practice was not dissimilar in terms of matching to fostering, with some hope of support into adult life:

When we have had good matches it's worked very, very well and when we have had the supported lodgings host move that person on, kind of building that nurturing relationship and being there for that person, attending reviews and into their independent living, that relationship has often remained after the supported lodgings. (Leaving Care Manager, focus group)

In our interviews with young people in supported lodgings and semi-independent living, there was a very great variation between those young people who were fully engaged in education or training and had very reliable support available to them, in some cases 24 hours a day, and those who were drifting and felt very isolated. This is discussed in more detail in Chapter 7, but it was clear that only a careful individual assessment/discussion with the young person would indicate what level of support was needed.

Intervention

Both LAC services and YOS nationally were able to describe a wide range of interventions for young people known to be offending and these were discussed in more detail through the focus groups. Most interventions are designed by the YOS to address the youth offending population in general, but are discussed here in terms of their particular relevance and effectiveness for young people in care.

Mental health/therapeutic interventions

There were a number of concerns about unrecognised, undiagnosed and untreated mental health disorders among looked after children who were also offenders, and this inevitably raised concerns about both assessment and screening processes and the availability and targeting of therapeutic resources. Specialist CAMHS support for LAC services and YOS seemed to be available in some though not all local authorities, with looked after children being rated high risk/high need by YOT staff:

> I think if you look within a needs-led approach, which I think we do around our interventions, because their needs are higher, looked after children actually get more resources because they tend to score higher, they tend to fall into the more intensive bandings – a generalisation, but they tend to have more complicated needs so they have more detailed plans around what's happening for them. (YOT, focus group)

Engaging these young people in therapeutic work was seen as a particular challenge:

> Generally speaking, we do have access to a range of different treatments, but young people that are linked into the YOT and connected to CAMHS are often very reluctant to engage and a lot of work goes into getting them engaged. The moment they see something as voluntary it's optional, so for us that's a bit of an issue, getting them to retain that engagement with us. (YOT, focus group)

> I think the issue as well is that our young people are reluctant to engage in therapeutic services, especially when we want that as adults because we want that placement to succeed. I think we need to think carefully about a continuing service and how whether that's via the foster carer, social worker, group meetings, and whether we are reaching the young person. (LAC, focus group)

For some practitioners, the concept of therapeutic treatment needed to be extended to include the placement environment:

I think some of it's the label we attach to things and "therapeutic environment" can be the environment of the foster carer and the high level of support. If you tell a young person they need a "therapeutic intervention" they go 'Woah!'. (LAC, focus group)

One local authority had used multi-dimensional social learning models of intervention (i.e. Multi-Systemic Therapy – MST) to help prevent admission to care and was keen to see Multi-dimensional Treatment Foster Care (MTFC) rolled out as a way of working with young offenders in care. Another local authority commented that it was not enough to have time-limited treatment placements that treated challenging behaviour if the young person had no family placement to go to afterwards and was drawn back to the birth family:

If at the end of that placement you have managed your anger, but you haven't got a family to live with, you still feel this tie back home. (LAC, focus group)

The complex and ongoing nature of most emotional and mental health problems, often combined with difficulties with communication and learning difficulties, required an awareness in all of the various organisations that are concerned with looked after children who offend or are at risk of offending. There are risks in adolescence of the triggering of genetic and other vulnerabilities to mental health disorder that exist alongside and may contribute to risks of offending. Conduct disorder and anxiety/depression are often co-morbid.

But alongside concerns about mental health, there were concerns about systemic issues that might also be affecting outcomes for looked after children:

Certainly a couple of years ago we had a higher breach rate among the looked after children than we did among the rest of the youth offending population. That was something, not just about their personal trauma and vulnerability, but it was something about the organisation and infrastructure between the YOT, the social worker and the looked after staff. (YOT, focus group)

Victim empathy and restorative justice

The review of the literature on risk of offending (above) highlighted the major role of social cognition and the link to affect regulation, pro-social behaviour, moral choices and restorative justice.

Concerns about social cognition and empathy have led to the development of victim empathy groups for adult offenders, and they were also described as one of the interventions available to YOTs. The groups are designed to enable young offenders to reflect on the thoughts and feelings of victims in ways which go beyond those particular individuals and which have the potential to shift the young person's capacity to tune into the minds of others in all relationships. One example is a programme by Wallis *et al* (2010), titled *What have I done? A victim empathy programme for young people*, and is explicitly seen as a foundation for using restorative justice. Strategies for promoting empathy can build on a range of interventions designed to promote what is also more broadly called "emotional intelligence", which have emerged from concerns around tackling bullying in schools.

Since, as reported earlier, there are several concerns about the capacity of looked after children who have experienced abuse and neglect to engage in and benefit from restorative justice approaches because of their lack of "mind-mindedness", strategies for promoting the development of social cognition among younger children in foster and residential care need to be a focus of attention long before children become at risk of anti-social behaviour and offending. For those who come into care as adolescent offenders, there needs to be a concerted effort by both YOT and LAC workers, as well as foster carers and residential workers, to address these problems in reflecting on their own thoughts and feelings and the thoughts and feelings of others, as this will affect all aspects of relationships and behaviour.

Education, training and activities

There have been policy-driven initiatives to promote the education of looked after children, with some success, but also some acceptance that, for many young people coming into care at 14 to 16, it is very difficult to reverse educational disadvantage. As the risk of offending and re-offending is likely to increase when young people are not engaged in education, employment or training (NEET) or not involved in any constructive activities, this was a concern for all practitioners. It can be classed as an issue for both prevention and intervention. At the earlier stages of prevention, there had been schemes to ensure smooth transition to secondary school, which had been subject to budget cuts. The need to avoid exclusion from school was an important focus, with restorative justice approaches being tried alongside the work of school-based police officers. In one local authority, this school-based work was described as successful.

> *It's been more successful latterly in the schools, because the policing policy within schools is about diverting children away from the criminal justice procedure and dealing with them in a restorative way. Now since we have the Safer Schools officers, which was approximately two years ago, that's been something we have been keen to pursue and make those specialist officers the gatekeepers of the policy within the schools.* (Police, focus group)

For the older teenagers at risk, one local authority described having put significant resources into specialist teams to reduce the number of NEET young people, including those in contact with the YOT and those looked after. Organisations in the voluntary sector that provided activity-based interventions for offenders and LAC were often able to link these to motivating young people to take a pride in themselves and to gain hope for the future, which increased the chance of moving them into college or employment.

As we saw from the files and the interviews with young people, the role of further education colleges was highly significant in offering an opportunity for young people, many of whom had been out of education for some years, to (re)discover education and career aspiration in an assisted adult learning context through academic and vocational courses.

Work with birth families

Although not a major and direct focus of discussion, there were concerns that much more work needed to be done with the birth family both to build positive relationships where they were possible and to protect young people from risk that might flow from some close ties to anti-social or emotionally demanding families.

Professional anxiety that young people in foster or residential care would be drawn back to the birth family, either in the role of caregiver for vulnerable parents or siblings or simply because there was nowhere else to go, was very strong. A CAMHS psychologist in one of the focus groups commented:

> There's also this kind of what feels like toxic magnetism back to the family of origin. The young person has been moved from quite a chaotic, quite a destructive family environment, and I think we don't pay enough attention to the contact that continues. A lot of the young people I have worked with have retained the relationship with the family of origin, even when they have been adopted in one case that I can think of. There's a lot of intervention going around the young person, but from a CAMHS perspective, not enough work with that biological family as well. (CAMHS, focus group)

This work was also deemed important for those in residential care, as this children's home manager described:

> We work very much with the families, where there is a family present. When children come into care, the families have often washed their hands of them. Very often if we can repair that, we try to. It can vary. Some children have excellent relationships with their birth families, they visit regularly, they go home for weekends, but they just can't live together. But we do have other

children where the parents at this time don't want to know, which is very hard for the child. (Residential Manager, focus group)

When we think of children's long-term care placements, we need to bear in mind the place that the birth family will continue to have in the mind of the young people and potentially in their lives. The role of the birth family may in the long run prove to be supportive or may add to their difficulties and risk of offending, depending on the quality of social work with parents as well as the young people themselves (Schofield *et al*, 2010; Schofield and Ward, 2011).

Tackling substance misuse

Many of the young people interviewed spoke about drug use as an important part of their life, but the issue was not discussed much in the survey nor did focus group members raise it until we did. The reason offered by focus group members for not having mentioned drugs was in itself significant:

I think it's fair to say we are desensitised to substance misuse. I wouldn't say it was the norm but a very high percentage of the kids that come to us use drugs. I think they are self-medicating, most of them, and know they are doing that to blot out the horrors of their past. (YOT, focus Group)

There were interventions designed to help young people/young offenders reduce their substance use, but this is clearly an area in which those involved with looked after children need also to gain expertise in order for the contributing risk factors and the risk consequences to be managed more effectively (see Chapter 7 on young people's narratives).

The importance of timely interventions

It was clear from the discussions of these various issues and interventions that practitioners are aware of a vicious circle in which school failure, instability in care and offending combine to increase risk. But there was also hopefulness and a sense of the opportunity for a virtuous circle, in which intervention at crisis or transition points could provide stable care, enhance educational opportunity and reduce the risk of offending or re-offending.

What is clear is that time is rarely on the side of looked after children. Whether they are five years old and already suspended from school for violence towards other children, or teenagers with a history of offending, an intervention to prevent momentum building towards a destructive pathway that will be hard to reverse is essential.

Transition to adulthood

Various sections above, such as the discussion of residential care, have highlighted aspects of "leaving care" that may add protection or risk of offending to a young person's pathway into adulthood. It was acknowledged that the transition to adulthood for young people will be affected by the characteristics of the young person and their history, but also by features of both the care and the youth justice system. Both survey respondents and focus groups acknowledged with concern that most young people need some kind of support from the teenage years into their early twenties and that this group was particularly vulnerable during this period if support was not available. It is an area of practice which was brought into greater focus by the Children (Leaving Care) Act 2000, but where practice remains problematic for reasons that are often, though not only, about resources (Stein, 2012).

For looked after children who were also at risk of or had a history of offending, concerns were raised about the particular risks of early moves from the care system into semi-independence or independence. These young people were often immature and vulnerable, but also lacked social capital in the form of supportive networks of family and friends, and indeed were likely to have or find risky networks. As discussed above, the majority of young people with significant histories of offending are likely to be in residential care and it is residential care that is likely to lead to relatively early moves from their placement in the teenage years. Practitioners commented that, in the crucial adolescence period, even 12 to 18 months of further work and enough support/time to mature can make a difference, e.g. moving into semi-independence at 18 rather than at 16½. Not all young people will be willing to stay on in foster or residential care and some prefer/may do better in semi-independent accommodation. But this move needs to be based on the young person's needs and wishes rather than on resources. And young people may need to return, after leaving, as they would to a family home, if they cannot cope.

Local authorities described quite varied structures for delivering support to care leavers/young people in transition and these also varied in the extent to which they addressed the risk of offending. This variety would affect the experience of looked after young people involved in the youth justice system. Following the series of initiatives on leaving care culminating in the Children (Leaving Care) Act 2000, most local authorities set up "leaving care" or "after care" teams with the provision of "personal advisers" to support young people with the emotional and practical tasks of moving into semi-independent or independent living. These teams may operate within the local authority or may be commissioned from the voluntary sector, but tend to pick up children at the review before their 16th birthday. The voluntary organisation service in one of the four focus group local authorities was described as working well, especially in being required to track and work with young people placed out of the area. They also had responsibility for the mediation and restorative justice service and for providing activities, thus operating across a range of other services and working with social care and youth offending staff. The importance of longer-term support was emphasised:

> *Educational outcomes are poorer, holding onto stable accommodation is poorer, having stable relationships are poorer – so a high probability is that they are going to remain vulnerable to offending for longer than other young people who have gone through those difficult transitions.* (Leaving Care Manager, focus group)

Some local authorities described having an "adolescent and after care team" that included children from 13 to 18, and was introduced to offer continuity and avoid young people transferring to a "leaving care" team at 16. Within this system, personal advisers worked along-side case responsible social workers with 16- to 18-year-olds, taking responsibility as key worker when the young person was 18. To meet the needs of care leavers living independently, one London Borough also provided a staffed drop-in centre for young people to come to during the day, which was very well-attended.

A series of practice examples were given by survey respondents to capture something of the services they valued. For example:

Projects like 'Making it Work' are advantageous, because they deal with life skill shortage issues and advocate to get young people into purposeful activities, employment, and routines of behaviour that are positive. Access to therapeutic intervention and work on issues of self-esteem are also important in encouraging young people to move on from negative life situations. (Leaving Care Manager, English Metropolitan Council, survey)

And the dilemmas they faced in meeting the needs of very different young people:

Taking a chance on a young person to provide a flat and a space of his own. Care leaving team felt that it was worth giving him a chance. Although he was 16 years old, he had caused a lot of damage and committed offences in every other placement he had been in and had not used the support. He had said he wanted his own place, but initially we all felt he was too young, would be taken advantage of, and would use the flat as a centre for anti-social and criminal behaviour. However, after all other options had been tried, the personal advisor assessed that it was worth a go to test him out. Since the move, he has accepted the support and there has been a significant reduction in offending behaviour and an increase in engagement. (Leaving Care Manager, English Unitary Council, survey)

We have recently had a young person late into care as a result of a serious offence and he was very quickly into his 18th birthday. However, because of his Schedule 1 status, placement stability was essential to help engage the young person in completing the treatment programme. We supported his continuing place-ment in one of our schemes and to support him there while he completed his treatment programme with YOT and engaged in some developmental work. We are also working on plans together with move on plans at a slow pace to ensure he is a) safe b) supported and c) as a result of the work, that he is as safe as possible in the community. (Leaving Care Manager, English Unitary Council, survey)

As described by these practitioners, and reported by young people in the study, the experience for older young people in contact with care and youth offending systems is of relationships with a number of professionals, sometimes with overlapping roles and sometimes with the experience of a reduced service as they get older. However, there are also opportunities to be creative, through listening to the young people, building relationships and working closely together to maximise support.

In the youth justice system, the shift from the youth offending team to the probation service at 18 was universally described in the focus groups as a step down from the kind and level of support that was available from the YOS. Although the two services worked together closely in some areas to ensure smooth transitions, with information about young people made available to probation staff, this reduction in support might also affect the young person's sense of security.

The LAC pathway planning system, based on the six-monthly reviews, is intended to ensure that young people are appropriately supported in all aspects of their lives, so it is likely to be within this system – with the support of the IRO – that some co-ordination of effort within and between both care and youth justice services should be achieved. This is in fact required in the care planning and care leaver regulations and guidance (DCSF, 2010a, b).

123

Interagency working

All topics discussed above needed some focus on interagency working, whether between residential workers and the police or LAC social workers and YOT workers or social workers and mental health services. Some of these working relationships are based on protocols and guidance (e.g. regarding responses to anti-social behaviour in residential care), but most are not. Nevertheless, the principle of inviting LAC and YOT workers to each others' planning meetings, where appropriate, was common and the degree of flexibility was welcomed. No one was asking for attendance to be required, since it was not always appropriate or desirable to have every professional involved in a young person's life at their LAC review, for example.

For the most part, there seemed to be a strong sense of goodwill between agencies described in the focus groups, although as each agency was facing pressure on their resources, there was also concern that some joint initiatives were under threat, especially in the area of prevention and training, but also in terms of setting up teams of specialist workers or specialist placements.

Some concerns were expressed that the very fact of pressure on the resources of individual agencies needed to be taken into account when planning the mechanisms for interagency working. The expectation, for example, that social workers from the youth offending and social care services should attend a series of meetings at the YOI – in itself a good idea but in addition to LAC reviews and YOS meetings – was seen as taking time away from direct work with and on behalf of young people and so needing extra resources.

Working together was often not only about working with agencies in stable relationships in a local area, but working with other agencies in areas where children were placed – which meant very rapidly trying to develop a relationship of trust with unfamiliar people and agencies. While some leaving care services reported a good relationship with YOTs outside their local authority, survey respondents were more likely to state that problems with poor communication and information-sharing created barriers to successful working relationships. This included difficulties with acquiring information, YOS omitting to invite leaving care staff to meetings, and queries over who was responsible for various aspects of the young person's life, including engaging his or her participation. It was also felt by one local authority that their young people who moved to another borough were not prioritised by the local YOS:

> *Contacting and working effectively with YOS workers in other local authorities can be challenging due to distance and the fact they do not always prioritise young people from other local authorities.* (LAC, Unitary Council, survey)

> *There are authorities that will not accept any responsibility or offer any support to young people from outside of their authority.* (YOT, Welsh County Borough Council, survey)

As discussed at the beginning of this chapter, strategies for reducing the risk of offending by looked after children are inevitably going to be multi-disciplinary and are likely to cross local authority boundaries.

Summary

- *Local authority policy, targets and strategies* for reducing offending by looked after children and preventing inappropriate criminalisation are widely but not universally in place. Some areas have multi-agency strategies established at senior management level, but many do not.
- Managers in both looked after children and youth offending services often lack *accurate and aggregated data* on which to base their joint strategic planning and monitoring of practice. The placement of looked after children outside of local authority boundaries in particular can affect tracking and service provision, especially specialist services such as mental health and education support. Joint working requires much better information gathering and sharing.
- *Assessment, planning and review* operate in accordance with national requirements (i.e. LAC and Asset) in both the care and

youth offending services. Both frameworks were found to be useful, but have certain limitations. In relation to looked after children and offending, it was suggested that the LAC review processes need to be able to pick up on concerns at an earlier stage. Both LAC and Asset need to pick up overlapping risks regarding mental health, learning difficulties and offending that would also be jeopardising placement stability. Some YOS teams talked of an increasing focus on assessing "vulnerability" as well as "risk", especially relevant for joint work with the LAC teams.

- Responsibility for *prevention of first offending* for looked after children was said to rely on good quality foster or residential care that mitigated the impact of abuse and neglect and could be protective against anti-social influences. But input/advice from YOT prevention services and mental health services may be necessary to prevent early conduct disorders/attachment problems escalating. There were examples of good practice in YOT prevention schemes that were not often being used to inform social work LAC practice.

- For *diverting* children who showed anti-social behaviour and *preventing re-offending and escalation of offending*, a multi-dimensional approach that combined relationship building, education/activities, and boundary setting was found to be necessary – but required a multi-agency approach that was better developed in some areas than others.

- Prevention of looked after children being *inappropriately criminalised* was a major issue. Restorative justice approaches combined with effective use of protocols between the police and residential staff were therefore seen as essential, and there were excellent examples of good practice at a local level. However, there seemed to be difficulties in ensuring that residential staff were trained appropriately and police engagement with the process varied. In addition, CPS staff were not always observing the relevant guidance regarding looked after children in residential care.

- *High quality and effective foster care placements* were viewed as able to provide stability, reduce risk and promote resilience, as indicated in the wider research. Foster care was perceived to be highly protective where secure attachments and stability were available and children's education and engagement with the community were promoted. There were some concerns about the availability of foster carers who could work with children at risk of offending when there was also a shortage of foster care. Some agencies also reported that because of budget cuts they were losing specialist adolescent fostering services.

- *High quality and effective residential care* was said to be most likely in small units with well-supported and trained staff, where other agencies, including the police, worked in partnership. Concerns about residential care were about ensuring adequate staff training and support.

- There were also concerns that in some agencies there was *pressure to move young people out of residential care placements early*, sometimes by their 17th birthday, into "semi-independence", often causing breakdowns in schooling and adding risk of offending. Supported lodgings and semi-independent living arrangements were seen as less suited to these most vulnerable young people, and yet they were more likely to be moved into them at a younger age than more competent young people in foster care.

- The experience of *looked after young people in the secure estate* caused some specific concerns, both in terms of maintaining contact with young people at a distance and in terms of managing their reintegration into the community.

- A range of *interventions* for young offenders was described, each with valuable implications for meeting the needs of young people who are also looked after, in particular, mental health/therapeutic interventions; victim empathy and restorative justice; education, training and activities; work with birth families; tackling substance misuse; and work on speech and language. For many young people, a multi-dimensional approach was required.

- The overwhelming message in relation to looked after children and offending was the *high-risk period of "leaving care"* and the difficulty in providing the necessary accommodation and support, including for education and employment, for vulnerable young people, especially where they were already at risk of offending. Some local authority and voluntary organisation provision was felt to be doing a reasonable or good job, but we cannot overstate the concern that practitioners feel for vulnerable young people expected to manage, in some cases, with very limited support.

- *Interagency working* was both a challenge and yet seen as essential in this area of work. Joint working at all levels seemed to be helpful, with the need to engage large interagency boards on this issue, but also the need for key advocates from YOS and LAC to work together at the most senior and the most junior levels.

5 Risk and resilience profiles of young people in the study

We wanted to identify risk and protective factors that are associated with increasing or decreasing the likelihood of offending by young people in care, based on the known research on risk and resilience factors predicting offending.

One hundred young people were interviewed across the four participating local authorities. The sample was designed to include a core group of looked after children who were in contact with the youth justice system (referred to as *LAC offenders*, n = 33) and two comparison groups – young people in contact with the youth justice system but not looked after (referred to as *non-LAC offenders*, n = 35) and looked after young people who were not in contact with the youth justice system (referred to as *LAC non-offenders*, n = 32).

The phrase "in contact with the youth justice system" was used to mean a young person who had received a referral order or above and had an Asset assessment undertaken, therefore indicating that the young person would have been convicted, appeared before a court, and have had a significant amount of involvement with the YOS. We requested that local authorities included young people who had committed a range of offence types, including those who had committed violent and/or non-violent offences.

The term "looked after children" was used to include young people who were looked after by the local authority through a care order or under section 20 (Children Act 1989). For young people who were looked after and who had offended, they needed to have the status of being looked after at the time they were referred to YOT. We requested that the sample of young people who were looked after had been so for varied lengths of time, but preferably at least 12 months prior to their contact with YOT and our interview. We sought young people who were placed in a range of placements, i.e. residential care, foster care, secure units, semi-independent and independent living.

We gathered data from file searches into Asset files (files maintained on each individual by youth offending teams) and care files (files on each individual in the care system held by children's services). We also gathered data from interviews with each young person in which we asked about their views on school, college and work; where they were living; who they were living with; what they did in their spare time; friends; offending; contact with birth family (LAC only); their experience of professionals; and what their plans were for the future. We also collected data on emotion recognition (using an instrument called the DANVA2 (Nowicki and Duke, 1994)); Attribution bias (using the Adolescent stories (Conduct Problems Prevention Research Group, 1999)); perception of behaviour and psychological adjustment (Goodman *et al*, 1998) and vocabulary knowledge (using the British Picture Vocabulary Scale – BPVS (Dunn *et al*, 2009)).

Using these data sources we identified risk and resilience factors across four psychosocial areas – individual, family, education and community – to compare the risk and resilience profiles for the three groups of young people, depending upon their care and offending status.

The sample

The aim of recruiting across different authorities was to obtain a diverse sample from urban and rural areas, including a London Borough. The groups were almost evenly spread across local authorities, but there was some variation. Our aim of keeping an even ratio of young people in each offending/LAC category group was achieved (33/35/32).

Gender

We requested a gender ratio of 70:30 boys to girls to reflect the higher proportion of boys in the offending population, but also to allow sufficient girls within the sample for qualitative analysis. The gender ratio was similar across the participating authorities, with 69 per cent (n = 69) of the sample overall being male; however, the ratio within each group did differ: the LAC offender group had 25 males and nine females, the non-LAC offender group had 28 males and seven females, while the LAC non-offender group had 16 males and 16 females.

Age

We targeted young people between 15 and 17 years old and achieved a range from 14 to 19 years. The mean age was 17 years 1 month. The age range of the sample was normally distributed.

The mean age for girls was 17 years 1 month, ranging from 15 to 18 years and 6 months, while the mean age for boys was 17 years and ranged from 14 years, 2 months to 19 years, 11 months. There was no significant difference in mean age between girls and boys.

Ethnicity

The sample included a range of ethnicities evenly distributed across all sample groups as outlined below in Table 9. The proportion of black and minority ethnic children within the general population of under 16s was 21 per cent in 2011 (Simpson, 2011). The proportion of black and minority ethnic children in the LAC population was 23 per cent in 2010 (DfE, 2010a). The proportion of black and minority ethnic children in the 10- to 17-year-old offending population was six per cent in 2009/10 (Ministry of Justice, 2011). Therefore, we have an over-representation of black minority ethnic young people in the offending groups, but a similar representation in the care groups. There were four asylum-seeking young people within the sample (3%) compared with five per cent within the national care population at 31 March 2010 (DfE, 2010a).

Table 9
Ethnicity across sample groups

	LAC offender	Non–LAC offender	LAC non-offender	Total
White British	67% n = 22	63% n = 22	63% n = 20	64% n = 64
Black and minority	33% n = 11	37% n = 13	38% n = 12	36% n = 36
Total	**100% n = 33**	**100% n = 35**	**101*% n = 32**	**100% n = 100**

* Due to rounding

Offending
Type of offence
All young people in both offending groups, LAC and non-LAC, had received a referral order or above, as this was one of the sample criteria. There was a wide range of offences across the offending groups, including violent offences, sexual offences, drug-related offences, gang-related offences and various theft-related offences. We requested from case study authorities that participant young offenders have a range of offence types. We coded offences as violent (against the person) or non-violent (against property). In the sample of offenders (n = 67), there were 37 per cent (n = 25) non-violent offenders and 63 per cent (n = 42) violent. When looking at the two offending groups, there was no significant difference between the LAC offenders and the non-LAC offenders in terms of type of crime.

Number of offences and rate of offending
Prolific offending has been a focus of government policy on offending in the last decade through targets to reduce recidivism (Home Office, 2002). The Home Office has made a distinction between levels of offending to identify those who offend the most. It identified prolific offenders as a small proportion of offenders who have committed a high proportion of all crime detected (Roe and Ashe, 2008). Prolific offenders have been defined as those who committed six or more offences within a 12-month period. It is these prolific offenders who would be likely to also fall into the definition of Moffitt's typology of life course persistent offender, as described in the literature review. In our sample of young offenders, the total number of convictions (by date of interview) for each young offender showed that they were clustered at the lower end of the distribution producing a median number of convictions of four; however, the other half of the offender sample was more spread out, with a wide range of five to 48 convictions recorded. There was no significant correlation with age, indicating that the number of convictions was not increasing as young people were getting older and that young offenders were just as likely to be prolific offenders as older offenders.

Although the national statistics (DfE, 2010b) indicate that there is a higher proportion of offenders within LAC populations compared to non-LAC young people, there is little evidence about offending rates within LAC populations. Higher proportions of young people obtaining a final warning or reprimand indicate a higher rate of contact with the youth justice system, but not the extent of offending behaviour within the LAC offender group or non-LAC offender group. While we did not record when each offence occurred, we did record the date of the first offence and that of the most recent offence which, combined with information on the young person's number of total convictions at the date of the interview, allowed us to calculate a rate of offending per year. The distribution of offending rate was positively skewed to low numbers of offences committed per year. The median offending rate for all offenders was 1.7 offences per year. The majority of the offending sample (94%) had committed fewer than six offences per 12-month period with only four per cent having committed more than six offences in a 12-month period, and therefore falling within the definition of a "prolific offender". There was no significant difference between the offending rates of the LAC offender group and the non-LAC offender group. Although this would warrant further investigation, the similarity of offending rates suggests that LAC offenders, although at risk of offending, are not necessarily at any greater risk of prolific offending.

Age at first offence

The mean age of first offence for the offenders was 13.5 years with a wide range from 10 years (age of recognition of offending by the criminal justice system) to 17 years. There was no significant difference in age for first offence by LAC status: LAC offenders had a mean age at first offence of 13 years and 7 months while non-LAC offenders had a mean age at first offence of 13 years and 1 month. Francis *et al* (2007) found, from a longitudinal dataset, that the earlier the onset of offending the greater the likelihood of a long criminal career. Ministry of Justice statistics (2010a) show that in 2009–10, the frequency of first reprimand, warning or conviction is higher for 14–15-year-olds and 16–17-year-olds compared to 10–11 and 12–13-years-old (Ministry of

Justice, 2010a). In comparison with these national offending figures, this sample of LAC and non-LAC offenders had an earlier age of offending onset than the average.

Individual risk and resilience factors and offending[4]

Table 10 shows an overview of the individual risk and resilience factors considered in this case study across the three study groups of LAC offenders, non-LAC offenders and LAC non-offenders. Each of these factors is examined in turn.

Impulsivity

From file search data we found that only 10 per cent of the sample had a formal diagnosis of Attention Deficit Hyperactivity Disorder (ADHD) and of those 10 young people, nine were offenders (five LAC offenders and four non-LAC offenders) and one was a non-offender. By examining the hyperactivity factor from the Strengths and Difficulties Questionnaire (SDQ) scores, which measured all young people's perception of their own behaviour, we found that there was a significant difference in SDQ scores for hyperactivity between offenders and non-offenders. Offenders reported a combined higher mean hyperactivity score of 5.2 compared to non-offenders who reported a lower hyperactivity mean score of 4.1.[5] There were no significant differences between the hyperactivity scores of LAC offenders and non-LAC offenders. In line with the risk literature, offenders in this sample are showing higher levels of impulsivity than non-offenders, regardless of looked after status.

---

[4] Note: all table percentages for risk and resilience show within group percentages, e.g. for mental health the percentage shows the different frequencies across offending and care groups out of the number of young people who reported mental health problems, not from the whole sample.

[5] A t-test showed a significant difference in hyperactivity scores between offenders (m = 5.2, sd = 2.2) and non-offenders (m = 4.1, sd = 1.8), t (2,98) = −2.434, p = .017

Table 10
Overview of individual risk and resilience factors

Individual risk and resilience factors	LAC offenders	Non-LAC offenders	LAC non-offenders	Total
Impulsivity (from SDQ)*	m5.03	m5.35	m4.1	
Mental health*	41% (n = 20)	25% (n = 12)	34% (n = 17)	100% (n = 49)
Conduct problems** (from SDQ)	m4.44	m3.89	m2.14	
Pro-social behaviour (SDQ)	m6.91	m6.51	m7.69	
Using alcohol and/or drugs**	48% (n = 28)	41% (n = 24)	10% (n = 6)	100% (n = 58)
Age at first offence	m13y 7m	m13y 1m	n/a	
Emotion recognition errors**	md13	md11	md9	
Hostile attribution bias	m3.00	m3.06	m2.84	
Benign attribution bias**	m2.54	m2.66	m3.12	

*Significant difference between groups at $p<.05$
**Significant difference between groups at $p<.005$

Mental health

Previous literature shows a link between the experience of abuse and neglect and subsequent mental health problems (McAuley and Davis, 2009). We recorded from the file search whether the young person had a current mental health diagnosis and also whether the young person was receiving services from CAMHS currently or had in the past. We created a variable which took into account all of these data and any young person with a mental health diagnosis or who had any contact with CAMHS was coded as experiencing mental health problems. Across the whole sample, almost half (49%, n = 49) had some record of mental health problems. When comparing across groups, there were more mental health problems among the two care groups compared to the non-care group: more LAC offenders had a record of mental health problems (41%, n = 20) than LAC non-offenders (34%, n = 17) who, in turn, were more likely to have mental health problems than the non-LAC offenders (25%, n = 12).[6] Young people in care in this sample were more likely to have mental health problems than those young people not in care. This is not surprising perhaps once family histories of abuse and neglect are taken into account, but we are unable to model causes of mental health problems here.

Perception of behaviour and psychological adjustment

The Strengths and Difficulties Questionnaire (SDQ) (Goodman *et al*, 1998) was used to measure young people's self-rated perceptions of their own behaviour. The SDQ has been used widely to evaluate distinct elements of both positive and negative behaviour and assess the psychological adjustment of young people, either through self-reporting or through peer, teacher or parent ratings. We were only able to gain young people's self-reported perceptions of their behaviour here rather than caregiver or teacher reports. It should be noted that self-reports are susceptible to social desirability bias. However, the SDQ has been tested for reliability and validity in all its forms on nationally representative samples and self-report scores have been found to correlate well with the teacher and parent ratings (see Goodman *et al*, 1998, for details). We also have an objective

---

[6]   A chi square test showed a significant difference in the proportion of young people who had a record of mental health issues between the LAC offenders group (41%, n = 20), the LAC non-offenders group (35%, n = 17) and the non-LAC offenders group (25%, 12), X^2 (2, n = 100) = 5.029, p = .04

measure of behaviour in terms of offending in the sample and can compare self-ratings of behaviour with offending and consider any discrepancies between hypothesised relations between self ratings of behaviour and group membership. We would expect to see higher scores for the difficulties domains in the offending groups and higher scores for pro-social behaviour in the non-offending group. Five factors of behaviour are measured: emotional symptoms; conduct problems; hyperactivity/inattention; peer relationship problems and pro-social behaviour. All young people completed the 25-item questionnaire. From Figure 3 below we can see the scores across all three study groups compared to both British norms (Meltzer *et al*, 2000) and also the borderline cut-off scores that serve as an indicator for mental health problems.

For *total difficulties* scores, all groups were above the British norm level of 10.3 and below the borderline cut-off level of 16. The two offending groups scored higher (LAC offenders, m = 14.88; non-LAC offenders, m = 14.23) than the non-offending group (m = 11.62) for total difficulties scores. For *pro-social behaviour*, the LAC non-offenders scored highest (m = 7.69) compared to the two offending groups (LAC offender, m = 6.91; non-LAC offenders, m = 6.51). The LAC non-offender group was approaching the British norm score of 8 and were well above the borderline cut-off level of 5. For *emotional symptoms*, all three groups scored similarly (LAC offenders, m = 2.56; non-LAC offenders, m = 2.69 and LAC non-offenders, m = 2.94) and were also well below the borderline cut-off score of 6 and similar to the British norm score of 2.8. For *conduct problems*, the two offending groups had higher scores (LAC offenders, m = 4.44; non-LAC offenders, m = 3.89) than both the non-offender group (m = 2.14) and British norm score of 2.2 and also were at the borderline cut-off score level of 4. For *hyperactivity*, the two offending groups again scored higher (LAC offenders, m = 5.03; non-LAC offenders, m = 5.35) than both the non-offender group (m = 4.1) and the British norm score of 3.8, but did not reach the borderline cut-off level of 6. For *peer problems*, all groups scored higher (LAC offenders, m = 2.91; non-LAC offenders, m = 2.31, LAC non-offenders m = 2.28) than the British norm score of 1.5, but none reached the borderline cut-off

Figure 3
Strengths and difficulties scores by group

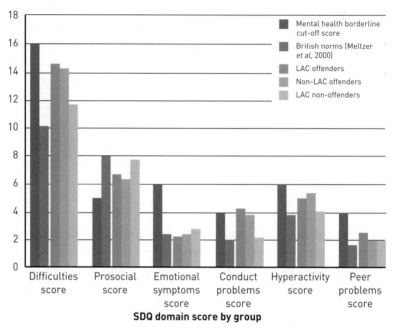

level of 6. When examining statistically significant differences across study groups, a series of comparison tests shows that the only statistically significant scores on the SDQ between study groups exists for *conduct problems*, where both offending groups have higher scores (LAC offenders, m = 4.44, sd = 2.25; non-LAC offenders, m = 3.89, sd = 2.01) than the LAC non-offending group (m = 2.14, sd = 1.60).[7]

---

[7] Assumptions for MANOVA were not met, so a series of ANOVA tests were conducted and a Bonferroni adjustment was made ($p < .007$) to account for type I error. ANOVA tests showed that there were differences between groups on conduct problems ($F_{(2, 97)} = 11.986$, $p = .001$). Post-hoc Bonferroni tests showed significant differences in conduct problems scores between LAC offenders (m = 4.44, sd = 2.25); non-LAC offenders (m = 3.89, sd = 2.01) and the LAC non-offending group (m = 2.14, sd = 1.60), ($p = .001$).

Alcohol and substance use

From the file search, we recorded whether each of the young people used alcohol and/or drugs and found that a significantly larger proportion in the offending groups used alcohol and/or drugs compared to the LAC non-offender group. Forty-eight per cent (n = 28) of young people in the LAC offender group and 41 per cent (n = 24) in the non-LAC offenders group used alcohol and/or drugs compared to 10 per cent (n = 6) in the LAC non-offenders group.[8] Some of this alcohol and drug use was related to offences such as drug dealing, possession of drugs and stealing alcohol, while other use was described in files as associated with coping with emotional difficulties. When just comparing the offender group with the non-offender group, the odds ratio of 14 indicates that offenders were 14 times more likely to be taking alcohol and/or drugs than non-offenders.

Social cognition
Emotion recognition

Each young person completed the DANVA2 emotion recognition task (Nowicki and Duke, 1994) where they were asked to attribute one of four emotions – happy, sad, angry and afraid – for each of the 48 faces that they viewed for two seconds each, in turn, on a laptop. When analysing the number of emotion recognition errors made by the sample of young people, the median rate of such error was 10.5. When we compared recognition error rates across our three groups, the LAC only group of young people had significantly fewer emotion recognition errors (Md = 9, n = 33) than the offender groups combined (Md = 11, n = 67).[9]

There is evidence to suggest that aggressive young people tend to over-identify anger (Fairchild *et al*, 2009) and that children who have

---

[8]   A chi square test showed a significant difference in the proportion of young people who had used alcohol and/or drugs between the LAC offender group (48%, n = 28), the non-LAC offender group (41%, n = 24) and the LAC non-offenders group (10%, 6), X^2 (2, n = 100) = 31.608, p = .001

[9]   A Mann Whitney U test showed that the LAC non-offenders had significantly fewer emotion recognition errors (Md = 9, n = 33) than the offender groups (Md = 11, n = 67, U = 841.50 , z = -1.941 , p = .028

experienced abuse and neglect have emotion recognition deficits (Pollak *et al*, 2000). We compared recognition errors across each of the four emotions and found that the offending groups showed more errors (Md = 5, n = 67) in mistaking either happy, sad or fear for anger than the LAC only group (Md = 4, n = 33).[10]

However, we also found a significant difference between male and female scores. Females (Md = 10, n = 31) had fewer emotion recognition errors than males (Md = 11, n = 69).[11] When just comparing offenders with non-offenders, we saw that offenders had lower emotion recognition scores than non-offenders. We also found that males have lower scores than females; we were therefore concerned that the offending group effect on emotion recognition may have been caused by the higher number of females in the non-offending group, so we tested for this possibility – see Table 11. We found that the differences shown by the offending group on emotion recognition appeared to be different depending on gender. For *female offenders*, there was no significant difference between the proportion of good (47%) and poor scorers (53%) in emotion recognition; however, there was a large significant difference in emotion recognition for *female non-offenders*. The proportion of good (100%) and poor scorers (0%) in emotion recognition for female non-offenders showed that all the female non-offenders were in the good emotion recognition scoring group.

For males, this pattern of emotion recognition was the opposite – *male offenders* were more likely to be in the poor emotion recognition group (62%) compared to the good emotion recognition group (38%), whereas there was no significant difference between *male non-offenders* for emotion recognition, with 44 per cent in the good emotion recognition group compared to 56 per cent in the

---

[10] A Mann Whitney U test showed that the LAC non-offenders had significantly fewer errors in mistaking happy, sad or fear for anger (Md = 5, n = 33) than the offender groups (Md = 4, n = 67, U = 654.5 , z = –3.244 , p = .001

[11] A Mann Whitney U test showed that females (Md=10) had significantly fewer emotion recognition errors than boys (Md = 11). U = 705.50 , z = –2.722 , p = .006, r = 27

poor emotion recognition group. Good emotion recognition appears to be more prevalent for female non-offenders than male non-offenders, and more of a problem for male offenders compared to female offenders.

Table 11
Interaction between gender and offending group on emotion recognition scores

Gender	Offender group	Good emotion recognition	Poor emotion recognition	Totals	
Female	Offender	(7) 47%	(8) 53%	(15)	100%
	Non-offender	(16) 100%	(0) 0%	(16)	100%
Male	Offender	(20) 38%	(33) 62%	(53)	100%
	Non-offender	(7) 44%	(9) 56%	(16)	100%
		(50) 50%	(50) 50%	(100)	100%

Hostile and benign attribution bias

Each young person completed the Adolescent Stories task (Conduct Problems Prevention Research Group, 1999), which measures attribution (interpretation of intent) bias. Young people were presented with six ambiguous everyday situations and asked to imagine themselves in the situation. They were then asked to rate the likelihood that the events in the situation were against them (hostile bias) or that the events in the situation were an accident or happened by chance (benign bias). From the literature on interpretation bias, which shows links between *hostile* attribution bias (interpretation of intent) and aggressive behaviour, we were expecting to see some differences between the offending groups and non-offending group. However, we found no significant differences between the three groups in hostile attribution bias (LAC offender, non-LAC offender, LAC non-offender). However, for *benign* attribution bias, there was a significant difference between the offending groups and the non-offending group. The LAC non-offender group had a higher mean benign attribution bias score (m = 3.12, sd = 55) compared to the group of offenders (m = 2.6, sd.54).[12] LAC non-offenders were more likely to attribute a benign intent in an ambiguous situation than were offenders.

It is interesting that there were no differences between hostile attribution bias between offenders and non-offenders; it would be useful to compare these groups with young people who were *neither* in care *nor* offenders to see whether having been exposed to more risks makes hostile attribution bias more likely in a high-risk population. Godwin and Maumary (2004) provide hostile attribution scores for their normative sample of young people from the Conduct Problems Prevention longitudinal study including hostile attribution bias (Conduct Problems Prevention Research Group, 2002). When we compared the standardised z-scores of the three groups in this study with the Dodge study, we found that the young people in this study had higher hostile attribution bias scores than young people who were *neither* in care *nor* offenders in the Dodge study. Dodge (2006) suggests that young people who have been exposed to violence at a young age are more likely to show hostile attribution bias as they have had to use this bias as a protective strategy while growing up. Widom (1991) also suggested that good quality care could provide a buffer between hostile bias and aggressive behaviour. It is possible that the LAC non-offenders in this sample were showing the protective elements of receiving good care because, while they showed hostile attribution bias, they showed benign bias as well. As Dodge (2006) indicates, benign attribution bias has to be socialised during childhood and so the carers of LAC non-offenders may have helped them develop benign attribution bias. If this is the case then we would also expect carers to develop benign attribution bias in the LAC offender group, which is not shown. If care quality is the factor that makes the difference in interpretation bias, then there may be differences in the care received by the LAC offender group, or it may be that the LAC non-offender group has a different risk profile to the LAC offender group. Examining the differences in care experience in this sample,

---

[12]   A t-test showed a significant difference between benign attribution bias scores between offender (m = 2.6, sd.54) and non-offender groups (m = 3.12, sd.55) $t (2,98) = -.4.443, p = .001$.

LAC offenders tended to enter care later, to experience more placements, and had stayed less time in their most recent placement, thereby suggesting that their care experiences were less permanent and more unstable and thus making socialisation of benign attribution bias less likely to occur. However, our measurement of care experience is not sophisticated enough to capture quality of care, so the link between care experience and the development of benign attribution bias needs further investigation in care populations.

Family and placement risk and resilience factors

Family structure for young people not in care
The majority of young people who were not in care lived with at least one of their parents (60%, n = 21). However, very few lived with both biological parents, and nearly a quarter of these young people lived independently or in temporary accommodation (see Table 12).

Table 12
Living arrangements for non-LAC offenders

Non-LAC offenders	n	%
Single parent	11	31%
Parent/step-parent	8	23%
Independently	5	14%
Temporary accommodation	4	11%
Extended family	3	9%
Both parents	2	6%
YOI	2	6%
Total	**35**	**100%**

Legal status of young people in care
Under the provisions of the Children Act 1989, young people can be looked after under a section 31 care order made by the court or under section 20, accommodation requested or agreed by the parents or requested by the young person. Young people aged 10 to 17 in care on a

care order are likely to have entered care at a younger age, while those accommodated under section 20 are likely to have entered care later. The majority of the young people in our care sample were on a care order (69%, n = 45), with the minority (31%, n = 20) accommodated under Section 20. When examining age at entry, those who were on a care order had a lower mean age (m = 8 yrs) at entry to care compared to those who were looked after under Section 20 (m = 14 yrs).[13] There were no significant differences in legal status between LAC offenders and LAC non-offenders, nor by age at entry and legal status between groups.

Table 13 shows an overview of the family-related risk and resilience factors considered in this case study across the three study groups. Each of these factors is examined in turn below.

Experience of abuse or neglect

From the file search we coded whether each young person had experienced physical abuse, emotional abuse, sexual abuse and physical or emotional neglect. There was a significant difference in the proportions of young people in both care groups that had experienced abuse or neglect. There were more young people in the LAC offender and LAC non-offender groups who had experienced abuse or neglect (38%, n = 16 and 48%, n = 20) compared to the non-LAC offender group (14%, n = 6).[14]

---

[13]　A t-test showed a significant difference in age at entry into care between young people who entered care through a care order (m8 yrs, sd 4 yrs) and young people who entered care through a section 20 order (m14 yrs, sd 3 yrs), t (2,44) = −6.531, p = .001.

[14]　A chi square test showed a significant difference between the care group (86%, n = 36) and the non-care group (14%, n = 6) in proportions of young people who had experienced abuse and neglect, X2 (1, n = 100) = 12.133, p = .001 (Yate's continuity correction used for 2x2 table).

Table 13
Overview of family and placement-related risk and protective factors

Family and and placement risk and resilience factors	LAC offender	Non-LAC offender	LAC non-offender	Total
Experience of abuse or neglect**	38% (n = 16)	14% (n = 6)	48% (n = 20)	100%*** (n = 42)
Negative parental influence	39% (n = 26)	31% (n = 21)	30% (n = 20)	100%*** (n = 67)
Age at entry into care* (entry up to 9 yrs)	35% (n = 10)	n/a	66% (n = 19)	101%ª (n = 29)
Main placement type**	Residential/ semi-independent	n/a	Foster care	n/a
Placement instability more than 4 placement moves)*	68% (n = 21)	n/a	32% (n = 10)	100% (n = 31)

* Significant difference between groups at *p*<.05
** Significant difference between groups at *p*<.005.
Negative parental influence = domestic violence, parental drug/alcohol use, criminal activity.
ª Rounded figures

Negative parental influence[15]

There are a number of negative parental influences that are outlined in the literature review in relation to increasing the risk of offending for young people. In this study, we recorded whether young people had witnessed domestic violence, whether their parents were involved with

---

[15] Note: that for file search records if there was no record of domestic violence, involvement with criminal activity, misuse of drugs or alcohol, this does not necessarily mean that the young person had not definitively experienced any of these issues.

criminal activity, and whether their parents had misused drugs or alcohol. In order to meet assumptions for our statistical analyses, we created one variable to indicate any negative parental influence across these three areas. There was a significant difference of experiencing some form of negative parental influence between the three groups: 39 per cent (n = 26) of LAC offenders experienced negative parental influence compared to 30 per cent (n = 20) of LAC non-offenders and 31 per cent (n = 21) of non-LAC offenders. The similarity of groups in experiencing negative parental influence is no surprise, as the majority of young people came from at risk family settings. It was the threshold of risk of such family settings which set apart the young people who were in care from those who were not in care; for example, as the results show, in their experience of abuse or neglect.

Age at entry into care

We noted the date of first entry into care and the date of the care order, where relevant, for each young person in care. Young people in care in this sample entered care across the age range from a few months to 16 years. However, when comparing age at entry across the LAC offender group and the LAC non-offender group, we found that more LAC non-offenders entered care before the age of 10 years (66%, n = 19) compared to LAC offenders (35%, n = 10). In this sample, LAC non-offenders were more likely to be early entrants into care.

Placement type for young people in care

Young people in care were mainly placed in foster care, residential care and semi-independent living (Table 14). Looking at placement profiles within the groups, the majority of LAC offenders were placed in residential care and semi-independent living while the majority of LAC non-offenders were placed in foster care.

The association of the non-offending group with longer-term foster care placements in this study supports a policy emphasis on achieving permanence in foster care placements. Many young people are moved on from residential care at 17 years, and are prepared for the move when 16. Moving young people who have experienced abuse and neglect towards independence at a relatively young age is ill-

Table 14
Placement type at date of interview: comparing total placement profiles by looked after group

Placement type	LAC offenders	LAC non-offenders	Percentage of total LAC group
Foster care	3% (n = 1)	56% (n = 18)	29% (n = 19)
Residential care	39% (n = 13)	9% (n = 3)	25% (n = 16)
Parents/kinship care	9% (n = 3)	9% (n = 3)	9% (n = 6)
YOI secure unit	6% (n = 2)	0% (n = 0)	3% (n = 2)
Semi-independent living	33% (n = 11)	19% (n = 6)	26% (n = 17)
Independent living	9% (n = 3)	6% (n = 2)	8% (n = 5)
Total	**99%* (n = 33)**	**99%* (n = 32)**	**100% (n = 65)**

*Due to rounding down

advised as evidence suggests that these young people are often developmentally delayed (Christoffersen and DePanfilis, 2009; Howe, 2011) and therefore need additional and longer lasting support through the provision of good quality care. However, providing semi-independent placements with good support is a positive option for some young people (see next chapter). Nonetheless, moving young people towards independence too early with not enough support is likely to contribute to an increased risk of offending.

Placement stability for young people in care

Sinclair *et al* (2007) found that both length of time in most recent placement and number of placements were associated with successful placements. Widom (1991) also found a connection between the number of placement moves and later arrest rates. However, this link was more likely in children who had entered care because of delinquency, in addition to abuse or neglect, thereby suggesting that the higher number of placement moves was as likely to be due to children's difficult behaviour as placement moves contributing to later offending. The young people in the LAC offender group tended to enter care later than the LAC only group. The advantage of admitting children into care earlier is that it is easier for new carers to influence the development of their behaviour. As children become older, anti-social patterns of behaviour are likely to be more habitual and more established and thus may be more difficult to change. Challenging behaviour may lead to more placement moves as relationships with carers are more likely to break down. For older children entering care, many placement moves are likely to be experienced as stressful and unsettling and are therefore hypothesised to have a negative impact on offending outcomes.

We assessed placement stability by looking at the time young people in care had spent in their current placement and the number of placement moves they had experienced during their time in care. From the file search we recorded the time each looked after young person had spent in their current placement. There was a significant difference between LAC offenders (Md = 6.5 months) who had spent less time in their current placement than LAC non-offenders (Md = 29 months).[16]

From the file search we examined the number of times young people in care had moved placements during their time in care. As the aim was to examine whether multiple placements were associated with offending, we measured the number of placements during total care period to date of interview. There were no significant differences between the LAC offender and the LAC non-offender groups on the basis of having had three or more placements during their time in care. Comparing LAC offenders with LAC non-offenders, using four placements or more, showed significant differences between the groups. More LAC offenders (68%, n = 21) had moved more than four times compared to LAC non-offenders (32%, n = 10).[17] The young

---

[16] A Mann-Whitney U test showed a significant difference in the time spent in recent placement between LAC offenders (Md = 6.5 months, n = 22) and LAC non-offenders (Md = 29 months, n = 22), U = 99, $z = -.3.36$, $p = 0.001$, $r = 0.5$

[17] A chi square test (with Yate's continuity correction for a 2x2 table) indicated a significant difference in the proportion of LAC offenders who had experienced more than four placements compared to LAC non-offenders, $X^2(1, 64) = 6.256$, $p = .006$

people in the LAC offender group had experienced more placement moves and spent less time in their most recent placement than LAC non-offenders, thereby indicating less placement stability during their time in care.

Education risk and resilience factors

Education is a particular concern for looked after children (Berridge, 2007). Education outcomes are one of the performance indicators that local authorities have to report each year for their children in care populations and those in care consistently underperform in comparison to the national population of children; for example, at 31 March 2010, 51 per cent of all looked after children had achieved five or more GCSEs at grade A to G compared to 92 per cent of the national population of young people (DfE, 2010b).

Table 15 shows an overview of the education-related risk and resilience factors considered in this case study across the three study groups. Each of these factors is examined in turn below.

Special Educational Needs (SEN)

From the file search we recorded whether any of the young people had a record of special educational needs (SEN). Out of 100 young people, 23 had a record of SEN. Of these 23 young people with SEN, seven had learning difficulties, nine had emotional and behavioural difficulties, three had both learning difficulties and emotional and behavioural difficulties, and four had no record of type of difficulty. We compared the proportions of young people with SEN across our three groups and found that the LAC offender group was more likely to have a record of SEN (61%, n = 14) than either the non-LAC offender group (17%, n = 4) or the LAC non-offender group (22%, n = 5).[18] Nationally the proportion of looked after children who have special educational needs is 28 per cent (DfE, 2010a). The figures we have here suggest

---

[18]   A chi square test indicated a significant difference in the proportion of LAC offenders who had a record of SEN compared to non-LAC offenders and LAC non-offenders, $X^2(2, 100) = 10.659$, $p = .005$

Table 15
Overview of education risk and resilience factors

Education risk and resilience factors	LAC offenders	Non-LAC offenders	LAC non-offenders	Total
Record of SEN*	61% (n = 14)	17% (n = 4)	22% (n = 5)	100% (n = 23)
Record of exclusion*	45% (n = 14)	48% (n = 15)	7% (n = 2)	100% (n = 31)
Difficulty with attendance*	45% (n = 21)	43% (n = 20)	13% (n = 6)	101%[a] (n = 47)
Qualifications*	26% (n = 10)	29% (n = 11)	45% (n = 17)	100% (n = 38)
Engaged with ETE*	27% (n = 20)	32% (n = 23)	41% (n = 30)	100% (n = 73)
Vocabulary knowledge (BVPS)	87 (20th percentile)	85 (16th percentile)	88 (22nd percentile	

*Significant difference between groups at $p<.05$. [a]Due to rounding.

that LAC offenders may make up a higher proportion of the SEN group among looked after children than LAC non-offenders.

Exclusion and attendance
From the file search we noted whether the young person had ever been excluded from school. The majority (69%, n = 69) had no record of being excluded from school. When comparing exclusion across our three groups we found that both offending groups were more likely to have been excluded from school than the non-offending group.[19]

When examining current behaviour we also recorded whether the young person was having any difficulties attending either education, training or employment. Out of the whole sample of young people 47 per cent (n = 47) were experiencing difficulties with attendance.

---

[19]   A chi square test indicated a significant difference in the proportion of LAC offenders and non-LAC offenders who had a record of school exclusion compared to LAC non-offenders, $X^2(2, 100) = 13.478$, $p = .001$

When we compared attendance difficulty across our three groups, we found significantly more young people in the offending groups (LAC offenders 45%, n = 21 and non-LAC offenders 43%, n = 20) were having attendance difficulty than in the non-offender group (13%, n = 6).

Qualifications

As noted above, the proportion of looked after children with qualifications is low compared to the national population of young people. From the file search[20] we noted whether the young person had any qualifications, including school and vocational qualifications. We considered young people in the sample who were 16 years or older (i.e. at an age when they would be taking GCSEs or equivalent).

There was a significant difference between groups for young people who had gained qualifications post 16 years: 26 per cent (n = 10) LAC offenders, 29 per cent (n = 11) of non-LAC offenders, 45 per cent (n = 17) of LAC non-offenders. The proportion gaining qualifications across all groups was below the national average of 51 per cent LAC gaining GCSEs. The main difference was between offenders (35%, n = 21) and non-offenders (65%, n = 17).[21]

Engagement in education, training or employment

From the file search we examined whether the young person was engaged at the time of the interview in any education, training or employment (ETE). Seventy-three per cent of the whole sample were engaged in some form of ETE. When comparing rates of engagement across our three groups, we found that more young people in the non-offending group (41%, n = 30) were engaged with education, training

---

[20] It should be noted that qualification in both Asset and care files is often under-recorded; therefore, these figures are likely to underestimate the number of qualifications held by young people in this sample.

[21] A chi square test indicated a significant difference in the proportion of LAC offenders and non-LAC offenders who had a recorded qualification compared to LAC non-offenders, $X^2(1, 71) = 3.132$, $p = .038$.

or employment than young people in either of the offending groups (LAC offenders 27%, n = 20; non-LAC offenders 32%, n = 23).[22]

Vocabulary knowledge

As established in the literature review, language has been found to be important for emotion regulation, which influences impulsive and aggressive behaviour, and offenders have been found to have low levels of language knowledge on standardised tests (Bryan *et al*, 2007). We wanted to examine the levels of language knowledge across our three care and offending groups. According to theory, all groups are likely to have some language development delay, but we would expect the LAC offender group to show most language delay.

We used the British Picture Vocabulary Scale (Dunn *et al*, 2009) to assess the vocabulary knowledge of young people in the study. The BPVS is a standardised instrument validated on nationally representative samples. There were no significant differences between the groups in vocabulary scores; however, all the groups were below the national norms for their age group and below the 25th percentile, meaning that mean vocabulary scores for young people in this sample were lower than 75 per cent of national norm scores for young people of a similar age.

Community risk and resilience factors

Table 16 below shows an overview of the community-related risk and resilience factors considered in this case study across the three study groups. Each of these factors is examined in turn below.

Positive activities

Gilligan (2000, 2009) outlined a rationale for the benefits of positive spare-time experiences for young people in care, which included the establishment of routine, self-discipline and a sense of purpose;

---

[22] A chi square test indicated a significant difference in the proportion of LAC non-offenders who had a record of engagement in ETE compared to LAC offenders and non-LAC offenders, $X^2(2, 100) = 10.505$, $p = .005$

Table 16
Overview of community risk and resilience factors

Community	LAC offenders	Non-LAC offenders	LAC non-offenders	Total
Taking part in positive activities	28% (n = 14)	20% (n = 10)	52% (n = 26)	100% (n = 50)
Having some positive peers**	20% (n = 9)	18% (n = 8)	62% (n = 28)	100% (n = 45)

*Significant difference between groups at $p<.05$. **Significant difference between groups at $p<.005$.

providing opportunities to meet positive peers and adults and widen social networks; and providing opportunities to belong to constructive social groups and developing self-efficacy. From the file search and qualitative interviews, we coded positive activities as being any constructive activity (e.g. leisure activity, sports, crafts, membership of groups) that was not education, employment or training. Fifty per cent of the sample (n = 50) were engaged in some form of positive activity. Across the three study groups, more of the non-offending group (52%, n = 26) were engaged in positive activity compared to the two offending groups (LAC offenders 28%, n = 14; non-LAC offenders 20%, n = 10).[23]

Peers

Contact with aggressive peers (Sinclair *et al*, 1994) and early social rejection from peers (Laird *et al*, 2001) have been linked to offending. From the file search and qualitative interviews, we evaluated any contact with peers as positive or negative. We coded positive peers as young people who were encouraging towards the young person's participation in education, employment or training; supportive to the young person in times of need; and discouraging of any anti-social or

---

[23] A chi square test indicated a significant difference in the proportion of LAC non-offenders who were involved in positive activities (52%, n = 26) compared to LAC offenders (28%, n = 14) and non-LAC offenders (20%, n = 10), $X^2(2, 100) = 19.686$, $p = .001$

criminal behaviour. We coded negative peers as young people who were themselves involved in criminal behaviour; encouraging towards any anti-social behaviour on the part of the young person; discouraging engagement in employment, education or training or other positive constructive activity; and those who were not supportive to the young person in times of need. As positive peers can be influential even in the presence of negative peers, we created two groups: one group in which there was evidence that the young person had contact with at least one positive peer and a second group where there was no evidence from the interviews or files of positive peer contact, but evidence of negative peer contact.[24] Using this coding, 47 per cent, (n = 47) of the young people had contact with at least one positive peer. When comparing peers across groups, we found that significantly more of the non-offending group had contact with positive peers (62%, n = 28) than the offending groups (LAC offenders 20%, n = 9; non-LAC offenders 18%, n = 8).[25]

Overall risk and resilience

Exposure to risk factors

From the risk and resilience findings (see Table 17) it would appear that young people in the sample were exposed to similar risk factors. However, when compared with each other, there was some differentiation between all three groups in exposure to risk.

Factors that differentiate LAC offenders from non-LAC offenders were the higher chance of experiencing abuse and neglect in the LAC offender group alongside their care experiences of more than four placement moves and entering care after nine years old. LAC offenders were also more likely to have special educational needs compared to non-LAC offenders. LAC offenders showed exposure to more risk

---

[24] We recognise that our data do not account for the entirety of each young person's experience of peers and therefore these findings should be treated as indicative of their social networks.

[25] A chi square test indicated a significant difference in the proportion of LAC non-offenders who had contact with positive peers compared to LAC offenders and non-LAC offenders, $X^2(2, 100) = 36.331, p = .001$.

Figure 4
Risk and resilience overview for case study groups

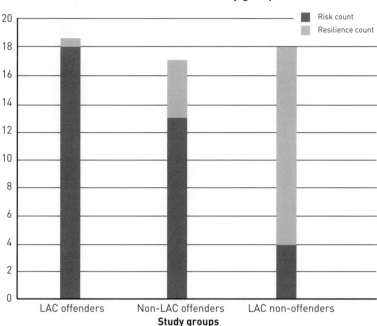

factors while LAC non-offenders showed greater exposure to protective factors (see Figure 4). In terms of care factors, LAC offenders were more likely than LAC non-offenders to come into care at an older age (10+ years), have more placement moves, and were more likely to be in residential or semi-independent placements.

Overall, LAC offenders had the highest risk count compared to both non-LAC offenders and LAC non-offenders, while the LAC non-offender group had the highest protective factor count compared to both the offender groups. These findings suggest that the different risk/protective profiles of each care group indicate that, while care can clearly be protective, by providing an alternative family for children who have experienced abuse and neglect, the care system faces the challenge to provide stable, long-term placements to young people

Table 17
Differences in risk and resilience factors between groups

LAC offenders	non-LAC offenders	LAC non-offenders
Impulsive	Impulsive	Less impulsive
Higher rate of mental health problems	Lower rate of mental health problems	Higher rate of mental health problems
Conduct problems	Conduct problems	Lower conduct problems score
Pro-social behaviour perception	Pro-social behaviour perception	Pro-social behaviour perception
Early age for first offence	Early age for first offence	n/a
Use alcohol/drugs	Use alcohol/drugs	Less likely to use alcohol or drugs
High rate of emotion recognition errors	High rate of emotion recognition errors	Lower rate of emotion recognition errors
Higher rate of hostile attribution bias	Higher rate of hostile attribution bias	Higher rate of hostile attribution bias
Lower rate of benign attribution bias	Lower rate of benign attribution bias	Higher rate of benign attribution bias
Residential/semi-independent placement	Family disruption	Foster care
More than four placement moves		Fewer than four placement moves
Into care after age nine years		Into care before ten years
Experience of abuse/neglect	Less likely to have experienced abuse or neglect	Experience of abuse/neglect
Negative parental influence	Negative parental influence	Negative parental influence

LAC offenders	non-LAC offenders	LAC non-offenders
More likely to have SEN	Less likely to have SEN	Less likely to have SEN
Exclusion from school	Exclusion from school	Less likely to have been excluded from school
Difficulty with attendance	Difficulty with attendance	Less difficulty with attendance
Less likely to have positive peers	Less likely to have positive peers	More likely to have positive peers
Less likely to be involved with positive activities	Less likely to be involved with positive activities	More likely to be involved with positive activities

Grey = risk factors. White = protective factors

who enter the care system later or those young people who have built up a high-risk profile.

Summary

Risk

- LAC offenders were exposed to more risk factors than non-LAC offenders and LAC non-offenders.
- Although the risk factors for both offending groups are similar, the LAC offenders were:
  - more likely to have been exposed to abuse and/or neglect;
  - more likely to be experiencing mental health problems;
  - more likely to have a statement of special educational needs than non-LAC offenders.

Protective factors

- Non-offenders had exposure to more protective factors than offenders. In particular, LAC non-offenders were more likely than LAC offenders:
  - to be in foster care placements;
  - to have entered care before the age of 10;
  - to have had fewer than four placements during their time in care;

157

- to have better emotion recognition scores, which was particularly marked for female non-offenders;
- to show benign bias.

Further research

These findings provide an insight into the likely risk and resilience factors for looked after children who offend. However, they should be treated with some caution due to the small sample size. We would encourage further research in this area to help explore risk and resilience in looked after children who are at risk of offending.

6   Risk and resilience: the narratives of young people in care

The focus of this project was on identifying risk and protective factors for young people in care in relation to offending. In the interviews with the two samples of young people in care, offenders and non-offenders, we asked them to describe their lives. In particular, we asked about what sort of positive and negative experiences they had and how secure they felt; how they were managing the various stresses they faced; and to whom they turned for support. We also used hypothetical stories of incidents in adolescent lives (Conduct Problems Prevention Research Group, 1999), which allowed us to access and discuss certain beliefs and expectations about the world (e.g. school, peers, the police). This chapter therefore focuses on what the young people said about themselves and their lives, drawing on theories of risk and resilience.

In analysing the interview data, the concept of resilience not only helped to identify young people's current capacity to manage difficult circumstances and find opportunities to fulfil their potential, but also helped us to understand what may have been protective in promoting resilience characteristics. It is possible to use the evidence of previous research to make connections with the various pathway factors (such as age at entry to care, type and stability of placement) and areas of functioning (quality of close relationships, engagement in education) that are likely to impact on risk and resilience in relation to offending.

The Secure Base model (Schofield and Beek, 2006, 2014), mentioned above and shown in Figure 5 below, highlights dimensions of caregiving linked to areas of child development that are significant throughout childhood. This model was used to assess, from a risk and resilience point of view, how well young people were managing their lives and the risk of offending – and the five child development dimensions provided a focus for the analysis:

- trust;
- managing feelings;
- self-esteem;
- feeling effective;
- sense of belonging.

These developmental dimensions are relevant for promoting security and resilience, but are also important for developing pro-social values and reducing the risk of offending.

A young person's *capacity to trust in relationships*, to have confidence in the emotional and practical availability of others, is essential to reduce anxiety and to enable them to cope with future challenges, to learn, to work, to have fun and to fulfil their potential. This is at the heart of Bowlby's concept of a secure base (Bowlby, 1988) and is relevant across the life-span, with the range of relationships able to provide a secure base growing and diversifying outside of the family in adolescence. The young person's capacity to mentally represent relationships as trustworthy is linked to their capacity to approach new relationships with the expectation that these will go well – and is associated with the social skills to increase the likelihood that they will.

The young person's capacity to reflect on their own feelings and the feelings of others is linked to the capacity to *manage* or *regulate their feelings* and therefore their behaviour. This capacity to think about your own mind and the mind of others is often referred to as *mentalisation*. It contributes to aspects of moral reasoning that are linked to the capacity for empathy.

Self-esteem and the young person's capacity to value themselves, try new challenges and manage setbacks increases the likelihood of engaging in constructive activities, which in turn builds self-esteem.

Feeling effective and having the confidence to plan, look forward and work towards goals are linked to self-esteem, but also to the hopefulness and aspiration that come from trust in others and in the future.

A *sense of belonging* and identity with a family (birth, foster or adoptive), peer group or community is of benefit to all young people, but is protective in relation to offending only if it offers support and promotes *pro-social values*. Where support is not available from these sources or needs to be supplemented, professional relationships are required that offer emotional, and practical support, but also challenge passivity or negative behaviour and offer guidance. Professional relationships too contribute to a secure base by reducing anxieties and can help build resilience.

Figure 5
The Secure Base model of security and resilience

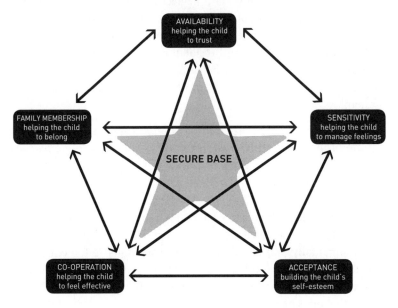

These Secure Base dimensions interact; for example, trust in relationships supports belonging, and self-efficacy requires the capacity to manage your feelings and behaviour. Thus, it is possible to see how the interaction of a looked after young person's trust in relationships, ability to regulate feelings, commitment to building self-esteem through education, self-efficacy and strong sense of belonging to a stable foster family will interact and reinforce each other in order to be protective in relation to offending. Similarly, it is easy to see how a young person feeling overwhelmed with anxiety and anger as a result of abuse and neglect, lacking pro-social moral values and the ability to feel empathy, having low-self-esteem and having a sense of belonging that is primarily with an anti-social peer group, experiences a combined set of difficulties that raise the risk of offending and make it challenging for professionals to intervene within or across the dimensions.

An even more complex picture emerges when we consider that young people will often have strengths in some areas but vulnerabilities in others – an important issue for those wishing to help young people who have experienced abuse and neglect in childhood, whatever the quality of subsequent adoptive, foster or residential care.

The history of resilience as a concept and in research suggests that no individual is so secure and resilient as to be invulnerable, nor so damaged or vulnerable as to be incapable of change for the better (Rutter, 1999). As Bowlby (1988, p. 136) put it, this is true across the lifespan:

It is this continuing potential for change that means that at no time of life is a person invulnerable to every possible adversity and also that at no time of life is a person impermeable to favourable influence.

The question then arises as to what combination of resilience and risk/vulnerability and at what particular stage in a young person's life (developmentally and socially) should professional interventions be targeted in order to shift a young person more fully to a positive upward trajectory that excludes offending. The promotion of resilience is the focus here (Rutter, 1999; Gilligan, 2000; Masten, 2001).

While many young people in our offending and non-offending LAC samples demonstrated a range of abilities and experiences on these dimensions, there were some patterns or pathways which are discussed in turn under three broad groups:

- resilient;
- coping with support;
- vulnerable and high risk.

Resilient

We are using the term *resilient* to convey the qualities across the five Secure Base dimensions that were demonstrated by certain young people in the care samples, mainly those without histories of offending. Not all young people were equally strong on all dimensions, but it was the process of interaction between dimensions, as resilience theory would suggest, that appeared to help them to function more effectively and pro-socially. Key here for young people in care was the capacity to reflect on and resolve feelings about the past, to move on and manage complex issues in the present, to be able to look forward with some degree of confidence in their own ability, and to hope.

It is important to remember that young people who were not offending were of course still vulnerable to certain kinds of stress and difficulty – including, for some, a degree of risk of offending – if circumstances were to change, or they were to lose key support or to suffer a setback in their aspirations. But these young people had developed some successful and flexible strategies for managing their lives. The majority in this group had never offended, though some young people with a history of offending but with significant individual qualities (such as being reflective and empathic) and with environmental resources (such as committed foster carers or excellent college support) had been able to develop resilience characteristics.

When considering the LAC interview sample who were able to show signs of resilience, we identified three different pathways (the ages given are age at interview).

Resilient: pathways and case examples

1. Young people who came into care under the age of 10, following often serious histories of abuse and neglect, and who had very quickly found a permanent placement in long-term foster care, remained there through to adolescence and were not offending.

Gemma (17) came into care at the age of seven. Her mother had mental health problems and Gemma had experienced significant neglect. She was placed initially in short-term foster care, but was in her current placement by the age of eight, where she has thrived in all aspects of her life and is part of the family. At the time of interview, she was studying at a college of further education and hoping to go on to university. She had limited contact with her mother and siblings. She had complete trust in her foster carers, high self-esteem, pro-social values and clear aspirations for the future. (LAC non-offender)

2. Young people who had come into care under the age of 10, and then had a number of foster or residential placements before ending up in a stable placement, often in early adolescence, where they were thriving. For most young people the final stable placement was in foster care, but there were some in final successful placements in residential care.

   Paul (15) came into care aged eight, following significant neglect and physical, emotional and sexual abuse. He had a series of foster homes and then a residential placement from which he benefited – and at age 12 was matched with a long-term foster family with a plan for permanence. He had learned to trust his carers and to regulate his feelings and behaviour, including adopting the pro-social values that were a key feature of this foster family and their community. He was at college and planned to work in a caring profession. (LAC non-offender)

   Gary (16) came into care aged four and remained in foster placement for some years before it broke down, as did a subsequent foster placement. After placement in residential care, at age 13, he initially displayed challenging and offending behaviour, but then settled in and since age 14 was stable with a pro-social friendship network. (LAC offender)

3. Young people who came into care in adolescence. Some had not offended prior to care and thrived in placement. Others had offended prior to care or offended soon after – but were now turning their lives around.

   Hannah (17) came into foster care at age 13 following a history of neglect. She had been very settled in this placement and at college, helped by loving foster family relationships and the fact that she was also able to maintain a positive relationship with her birth family. She spoke very warmly of social workers. (LAC non-offender)

Joseph (16) was an unaccompanied asylum-seeker who came into care at 14. His first placement ended when he committed an offence as part of a gang. He was now in a stable placement in a different area and committed to achieving in education. (LAC offender)

Resilient: trust in relationships
Trust in relationships relies on the belief that significant others will care about you as a special person and will be emotionally and practically available to you at times of need. These significant others in adolescence may be immediate caregivers (as in foster or residential care), a range of professionals (such as social workers, YOT workers, key workers for those in supported semi-independent accommodation, college lecturers, activity leaders), birth relatives or peers/friends/siblings. Each of these relationships has the potential to enhance the young person's capacity to trust and reduce their anxiety, and thus the potential to *provide a secure base* from which young people could explore their options, take up opportunities that arose, solve problems constructively, and build future relationships.

Young people in this group had experienced a range of positive and negative experiences in relationships, but were all able to name key people who had not only helped them to trust particular people but seem to have helped them to build a mental representation of adults generally as loving/trustworthy – matched with the resulting mental representation of themselves as lovable/worthy of love. This positive internal working model (Bowlby, 1969) tends to lead to relationship experiences that reinforce this positive set of expectations.

For most of these predominantly fostered young people, it was their foster carers who were the people they mentioned as being both the first person they would tell their good news to, and the person they would like to have by them if they were hurt or upset. These young people acknowledged the secure base effect they experienced, in that the loving care that was reliable and reduced anxiety was also associated with supporting exploration and age-appropriate competence:

It's good, they offer me lots of support and love and care; it's nice.

In what way, support?

Like when I was doing my driving test, they said I can do it and it helped me get through my driving test. (17, female, LAC non-offender)

The praise for their foster carers was often wide-ranging and in itself showed that they were able to trust in and see the value of relationships across diverse areas of their lives, ranging from emotional support to boundary setting and guidance. This example is from a young man who had been through a number of placements before settling happily with his current foster carers:

I praise [my foster carers] so much – you just cannot get any better, they are the best ones going.

What sort of things do they help you out with?

Just everything ... it's like emotional support, school life, education wise, friends, they help me to manage my money, how to live my life. They teach you all the basics and more. (15, male, LAC non-offender)

Especially powerful were statements suggesting that young people could reflect on and understand how loving and trustworthy relationships in care had provided positive experiences and role models and helped them to change:

I wasn't a good child because my birth family never showed me any love ... I was always angry, all the time, and then [foster mother] she saw what was going on and she knew, so she gave me love and she gave me what every mother should give their daughter and I changed my ways and now I don't do drugs or anything bad like that. (16, female, LAC non-offender)

Other young people also talked of special relationships and how these had changed their lives for the better. One 16-year-old boy had been in a settled, supportive and pro-social long-term foster home from soon after coming into care at age eight:

My carer [name], she's really nice and supportive and would help me through anything really. I've been here for seven years now. For me it's the best foster home I could have been to. She certainly helped me progress through school and everything. If I was ever in trouble and didn't know anything she'd always be there to back me up and ask why I done it and talked to me . . . She'd sit me down and say it wasn't a very acceptable thing to have done, what could you have done to be more positive? (16, male, LAC non-offender)

The open and trusting quality of this relationship was then reflected in his relationship with his foster brother. He was able to reflect on this constructively, including how "ups and downs" are normal in relationships:

He's funny – he's always up for a laugh and that. We have our ups and downs, but that's usual for any person that lives with each other day in day out. We share stuff like the X Box and everything and we never really get into any arguments that much and if we do we know we're big enough to sort them out and say, let's start again. (16, male, LAC non-offender)

This link between trust, sharing, compromise and problem-solving connects different resilience dimensions that were also evident in this boy's relationships with friends:

If there's ever a problem we sort it out ourselves, sort of thing. We can be quite close friends, our little group. (16, male, LAC non-offender)

For some young people, friendships were a key to their trust in relationships. Here continuity was important, but so also was the capacity to build new relationships:

> Yeah I do, I have all my high school friends and then friends that I used to hang around with in primary school and I keep in contact with them but just not as much, and then I have college friends. (17, female, LAC non-offender)

For some young people who went on to trust in foster carers, their experience of trust in a residential worker had been a turning point that perhaps made subsequent family placement possible. In this example, the secure base nature of the relationship with a worker (i.e. being encouraged to trust in order to explore) has a magical quality – and the interest in nature that it inspired in this boy continued throughout his adolescence. This is his account of a typical expedition with a residential worker to whom he felt close:

> One day, we went out about three o'clock in the afternoon and didn't get back until 11 o'clock at night. We walked for that long, so, like, we wouldn't walk completely to somewhere, we would get a train and then we would walk back. But we wouldn't go the normal ways, not the route ways on the road, we would go on all the woods and countryside, the little parts. It's amazing what's out there. Amazing, so much wildlife . . . There was seals in a river that goes out to the sea and it has this wall with all seaweed and a little bit of sand and he said, 'Here, look, do you think there's any life in them rocks?' and we would say, 'No, there can't be nothing', and then we used to go all through the rocks and find all this weird stuff like crabs and other stuff, it's just amazing. (15, male, LAC non-offender)

Key to the capacity to move on and trust relationships was the possibility of resolving feelings about difficult past relationships. For some young people, this was about having a different, more trusting, relationship with current carers that gave them the emotional skills which, in turn, enabled them to re-establish trusting relationships with their birth parents. This young person (16) came into care at age eight, following neglect and his mother's drug misuse. He was doing well at school and planning to join the police force. He talked of his improved relationship with his mother in adolescence, a relationship in which he is able to use his positive experiences to help her to share an understanding:

> We talk a lot more and talk about each other's feelings a lot more. We enjoy each other's company a lot more ... It's kind of like a mother and son situation, which is nice because I never had that when I was younger. Now that I'm older and I understand a lot more, it's reached a peak where we can trust each other and understand each other more. (16, male, LAC non-offender)

Resilient: managing feelings, mentalisation and moral reasoning

Managing feelings is key to managing behaviour. The significance of mentalisation lies in the young person's ability to reflect on their own thoughts and feelings and the thoughts and feelings of others. This means being interested in how their own mind and the minds of others work (Fonagy *et al*, 2002; Howe, 2011), as some of the examples above also show.

Mentalisation is linked in developmental attachment theory to "affect regulation", since an ability to reflect on and understand one's own feelings and behaviour and the impact they have on the feelings and behaviour of others is critical to regulating feelings, but also critical for then making choices about/regulating behaviour and becoming pro-social.

Mentalisation skills develop during the pre-school years in benign, sensitive parenting environments, and continue to become more sophisticated into adolescence, as other cognitive developmental changes occur, such as the beginning of abstract thinking. However, mentalisation skills may never develop even in adulthood for those who have not experienced sensitive care from caregivers able to be mind-minded and support the child's management of anxiety and exploration of feelings. This process of sensitive care and attunement is also key to helping the child to manage their aggression. Aggression is a natural expression of anger in early childhood, but needs to be securely contained, helping children not to feel overwhelmed and to find other ways to communicate strong feelings (Fonagy, 2003).

It was possible to see how the more secure and resilient young people were more subtle in their thinking processes. Unlike the capacity to trust, which is directly expressed in the *content* of young people's narratives, mentalisation is often apparent in both *what* young people say and *how* they say it (i.e. the choice of language, the flexibility in the thinking), which suggests a capacity to reflect. Very often, for example, it was possible to see that the young people were theorising, trying to think flexibly about why they and other people feel the way they feel or behave in the way they do. This is linked to the development of moral reasoning in terms of how this ability to understand and reflect on others' minds leads to an empathic response. But in addition, reflection on the self and others also leads to the necessary social emotions of shame and guilt. As discussed in previous chapters, restorative justice relies to a large degree on offenders' capacity to reflect on their own mind and the mind of the victim, and to have the capacity to experience both empathy and shame.

An understanding that other people could react differently in different circumstances was part of the flexible thinking that these young people showed – as well as an interest in how other people think. For example, this young person living in a successful residential placement felt that this experience had taught him to be more understanding and tolerant:

> *Residential care taught me how different we are as people in general, people's concentration skills. Because some people are slower to react to things the staff might say to them, and that's where you see some people explode.* (16, male, LAC offender)

What is clear from this kind of talk is that this is a young person who has not only learned about how other people think and behave, but has also now got the ability to put those ideas into words.

This comment not only suggests a more reflective way of thinking, but shows how this may be linked to a capacity for empathy that will inform all other aspects of their relationships, including their judgements on offending. One young person, when asked about what she might expect a typical offender to be like, suggested that stereotypes are unhelpful and individuals can be different:

I don't know. I don't think I would expect them to be anyone. Sometimes people can shock you because then you are stereotyping people. They would probably be the people you would least expect to do crime. (17, female, LAC non-offender)

This reflective way of thinking also emerged when young people were asked to think about what advice to give foster carers. As this other young person showed, her understanding of what children in care may have gone through emotionally and how foster carers should respond comes out in her advice to carers:

If there's a little kid and she's upset, just try to understand why. Don't think 'She's being horrible', 'She doesn't want to be here', 'She's ungrateful'. Understand that she has just been took away from her family and she needs love and support and everything. (17, female, LAC non-offender)

Young people's sense of how to express feelings often came through also in their response to the request to offer advice to young people:

Be strong but don't hide your emotions away, otherwise, if you hide them away and bottle it up, it will come out in a bad way. If you are upset about stuff, tell them, don't hide it. (17, female, LAC non-offender)

One of the areas we wanted to pursue with young people was their capacity to reflect on the impact of their anti-social behaviour and to consider links to their moral reasoning. This 15-year-old recalled making "prank" calls when he was younger, something he regretted when he realised the impact:

It made me not do it again, because the lady we did it to felt upset about it and I saw that and it made me feel bad. (15, male, LAC non-offender)

Young people described how, since being in care, they had become better able to manage impulses to be angry or aggressive:

People say 'You're an idiot' or bad words and I'd be like, normally I'd get angry and want to do something, but now I'm just like whatever, move on. Before I would have pulled them up and said, 'What do you want? What was that for?' and escalate into a fight and now I am just more laid back and doing good for myself. (16, male, LAC offender)

Even in this more resilient group, affect and behaviour regulation were often about resisting aggressive impulses in order to protect the self from their consequences.

As adolescents, these young people were at a critical turning point in terms of their thinking, *moral reasoning*, and committing themselves to a set of pro-social values that would be protective into adulthood. From the interviews, it seemed important to them to have a theory about why other young people offended – in itself requiring them to reflect on other minds – that was differentiated from their own thinking, circumstances and behaviour. So theories to explain why some young people may become involved in offending included linking offending to not being involved in positive activity, being at an economic disadvantage, or having a problematic past:

One of my friends who I went to middle school with ended up going to jail and I think it was his home life. He ended up burgling and went to jail for it, he was so fed up at home and had no money or anything. I think people do it when they want some attention; some people, if they don't get attention from anyone, or they need money, or if they had just had a really bad childhood and they think it is OK to do that. (17, female, LAC non-offender)

One young man (16), who had come into care young but became very challenging, had then settled into a successful placement in residential care in his early teens, which turned him around. He talked of the support he got from his YOT worker in terms of making him think about himself and his behaviour:

She made me realise that there is more to life than making money, fast money and being a young boss. I'll say, there's more to life than being a thug. (16, male LAC offender)

He described not wanting at first to get involved with sessions provided by the YOT worker to help him change his ways of thinking:

I used to put my head down – I'm not listening – until the fourth week of my ISP I just listened one day. From telling me how society sees people like us, like fugitives, and how we can change that and be better people and I started listening more and started educating myself through books and new music and the people around me and she helped me get out of that. I would give her big props [respect] for that. (16, male, LAC offender)

This example combines trust in the worker with a willingness to reflect and think about the choices this young person was making, which reinforces the capacity of young people to regulate their feelings and then builds self-esteem.

Resilient: self-esteem

The concept of self-esteem is a familiar focus for any assessment and intervention for young people. But self-esteem needs to be understood as a subtle concept – it is a resilience characteristic, but only when it is flexible, realistic and enables young people to cope with both success and failure. Young people therefore need a sense of self-worth that enables them to aspire to, achieve and enjoy success, but also to manage and move on from lack of success and setbacks without feeling that their core sense of self is threatened. As with all resilience dimensions, self-esteem is closely linked to and interacts with others, in particular, self-efficacy, but also family membership (whether foster family, birth family, or residential care), where how you are valued will be crucial to your self-concept and self-esteem.

These more resilient young people enjoyed looking back at their progress over time and saw self-improvement for the future as a challenge they were able to face. Some were aware of difficulties they previously had with education or employment, but had decided to face them or go into a setting that suited them better. Where young people had not liked school or had been excluded, they appreciated the autonomy that college or work afforded them. For example, the young man quoted below recognised that he was unsettled at school and had some attention difficulties, but he had found his niche at college and was more engaged:

> *I like learning new stuff and everything. It can be frustrating at times if I can't understand it, but that's what you're there for, isn't it? I like doing hands-on jobs helping people and I'd like to create my own stuff. I find I need to be doing something all the time. I couldn't just sit in an office. I have to be on the move, interacting with people . . . If all goes well I will get my plumbing certificates and everything I need and then try and find a job with someone, a company, and set off from there.* (16, male, LAC non-offender)

All of this group were involved in some form of education or training – and for some older teenagers, the role of further education colleges in providing education, training and direction to their daily life was crucial to their ability to engage with society as well as building their self-esteem. The colleges were obviously offering education to some young people aged 16 to 18 who had very varied and often unsuccessful previous educational experiences at school, or were unaccompanied asylum-seeking children who had gaps in their education, but were now getting another chance. The aim of developing skills was linked to confidence that this was achievable, as it might not have been previously possible because of their behaviour:

I wouldn't say I feel proud, but I can hold my head up high, same thing. I can say, yeah, I was like that and doing that and now I'm looking to do something for my future and now make peace. (16, male, LAC offender)

For most young people, constructive activity outside of education was also an important part of their self-esteem. Several young people were interested in martial arts:

A staff member was talking about it, so I looked it up on the internet, saw the way they fight, loved it, thought I'm going to try it and fell in love with it. (16, male, LAC offender)

Another young person (16), who came into care at age nine and remained with the same carer, said that she was involved with kickboxing and drama, and was working towards becoming a nurse. Others prided themselves on more unusual hobbies, or combined the new and the old, as did this 15-year-old boy:

Hobbies – I would say technology – I love it, can't get enough of it, anything new that comes out. One of my other hobbies is a Hornby train set, it's a collector's train set, not a children's – it's what people in their fifties buy. I have about three trains now, one of the trains alone is over £200! (15, male, LAC non-offender)

Previous research on children in care (Schofield and Beek, 2009) has emphasised the role of activity in raising self-esteem, often building peer relationships as well as contributing to confidence and self-efficacy. The focus on activities both in care placements and in the work of YOT teams is clearly justified, not just theoretically in terms of building resilience, but from research.

Resilient: feeling effective, self-efficacy

These more resilient young people felt in control of their lives, were confident of their abilities, and were proud of what they had achieved. They had positive, but again realistic, aspirations about the future. They were able to plan how to achieve these aspirations and had put the plans into action through attending college or gaining relevant employment.

This capacity to plan and to look forward is a resilience characteristic that links to both thinking skills and self-esteem. These young people were able to see the long-term benefits of working hard towards their goals and understood that this meant working with others co-operatively and sometimes compromising in order to achieve their objectives.

Again, these more competent and engaged young people had theories about how their own positive aspirations compared to outcomes of offending (including, for previous offenders, their own offences) and recognised that more personal fulfilment was to be gained through legitimate ways of bringing in an income:

> I like [college], it gives me loads of ideas about starting my own business and it helps me do loads of things ... If you want something, wait for it, you know? Because if you do these robberies and that, it ain't going to last forever, something will happen to you. But if you go proper to college and universities and get qualifications, and get a job, no one's going to take that away from you. When you own your own business and making money, you're making clean money, you get me? (16, male, LAC offender)

Young people could also articulate one of the principles of resilience – that successfully surviving bad experiences contributes to self-efficacy:

> That's just like loads of things happen, it makes you a bit stronger because being in bad situations, that makes you stronger. (16, male, LAC offender)

For some young people, self-efficacy was particularly clear in their attitude to their care identity and participating in their LAC review:

I think they're pretty helpful. I'm pretty confident and speak my mind, not swearing or anything. The reviewing officer, she listens to me, my school comes down, everyone's here basically and I get listened to. I tend to have them here [foster home] because I feel more comfortable here and I can speak more freely here than if I was in the school office or something. (16, male, LAC non-offender)

Self-efficacy is central to resilience and for young people who feel that they have extra battles to fight because they have come into care and have difficult family backgrounds, the message of hopefulness is crucial. This young woman's advice to young people in care was one of hope and aspiration in terms of changing from bad behaviour and offending to good outcomes:

Even if you are put in care, you can still have a good life, turn your life around, get grades and do what you want to do. Why risk it all for nothing? (18, female, LAC non-offender)

Resilient: belonging, identity and values

For looked after children, a sense of belonging is always complex and may include a range of families, friends and even professionals, all of whom may contribute to and shape their identity and values. Family membership may be one of the goals of permanence, but for adolescents in care, whether they came into care in early childhood and were placed in a long-term foster family that lasted or in an adoptive or long-term foster family that did not last, or only recently came into care in adolescence, family membership was complicated. Typically for looked after children, young people in this study had the full range of multiple memberships in care placements and with birth families.

For foster children, there may be uncertainty as to whether carers can or should be thought of as mum and dad, or be called mum and dad. This 16-year-old girl had been in her stable long-term foster placement since she was nine and she talked of her foster family relationships as being like any other family:

> *I have got my foster carer, who I see as my mum, and she has got an older daughter, who I see as my sister, and I have got all my siblings, my brother and sister.* (16, female, LAC non-offender)

She advised foster children to think about a foster carer as a mum, and linked this to the child's need to trust that someone was available:

> *Try and build a relationship with your foster carer, even though you may not want to, but this nice relationship just grows and she becomes . . . you feel like she is your actual mum, and it's just nice to have a relationship with someone, because you might feel like you are alone and you are not alone because you have got someone there.* (16, female, LAC non-offender)

One young person mentioned the fact that his long-term foster family had been formally confirmed as long-term through a permanence meeting in his local authority and this had been a special way for him to feel more securely part of the family:

> *I have definitely had over 200 meetings while I have been in foster care. But I have had the special, the most, best meeting you can have in foster care, a long-term meeting, getting a certificate saying you are long term in a foster placement.* (15, male, LAC non-offender)

Successful negotiation of family membership was often about managing relationships with both birth family and foster family members or residential staff. As in the examples given above, positive relationships with foster carers could often permit easy relationships with birth parents and birth relatives. One young man was very committed to maintaining his relationship with his grandfather, while seeing his foster home as "home":

I usually see my granddad once a fortnight if I can. He's 83. He used to be in the navy so that kept him fit and stuff. When I go down there we read the news, talk about stuff, maybe I'll watch a bit of telly, he reads his book and makes me egg and chips, and then I go home. (16, male, LAC non-offender)

A sense of belonging and identity for some young people was affected by their ethnicity, especially if they felt that this added to the stigma of being in care. This young person was black and growing up in a white area, so felt the need to challenge negative attitudes:

Some people think, 'Yeah, he's done well for himself' . . . and in secondary school some people were probably thinking, 'Yeah, he's a typical black guy, he's going to be up to no good . . .' (16, male, LAC offender)

Identity and pro-social values can come from friends, but some young people had to distance themselves from old friends:

They kind of crashed the party and me being me I was wary of these guys . . . My old friend K was there, 'Just chill with us' and I was like 'No, I'm alright'.

So you're not in touch with them now?

No, no, no, no, no. (16, male, LAC offender)

Young people in this group were able to discriminate between those social workers who they felt had let them down or been unreliable and those who had valued them, including providing practical support to keep in touch with their birth family and identity and listen to them:

She was brilliant, really good. It's a shame all social workers aren't like her. She got everything done, up to date, even drove my mum down to where I live and got all the core assessments done all in time and all my files up to date. She was generally a really good social worker and listened to me, which is what all social workers should do – listen to the child. (16, male, LAC/ non-offender)

Coping, with support

There was a group of young people who were currently stable in their lives and not offending, but who seemed to lack some of the resilience qualities of the previous group and were more dependent on their support networks. What is remarkable about their stories is that, although they were still vulnerable in some areas of their lives, with support, they were generally involved in education, training or some constructive activity, and for those who were offending, downward spirals appeared to have been halted. For this group we identified four pathways.

Coping, with support: pathways and case examples

1. Children who came early into care following maltreatment, but experienced a placement breakdown in adolescence that sparked a downward spiral into offending, which had stopped.

   Jennie (17) came into care at age two, following abuse. She was in a long-term foster family till age 12, when she found out about her birth family. Her behaviour became so challenging that she was excluded from school and the placement ended. She attributed her problems to struggling with being black in a white foster family, but had a profound sense of loss when the place-ment ended. Subsequent foster placements broke down and once she entered residential care there was a rapid downward spiral of increasingly serious offences, resulting in custodial sentences. However, she had not offended for three years. She was now well supported in semi-independent living. (LAC offender)

2. Children who came into care when older and following maltreat-ment.

   Suzy (17) came into care at age 12 after long-term neglect and alleged sexual abuse. She had missed out on schooling to care for her mother, who was drug dependent. She is retaking GCSEs. She spent four years in a foster family, but then became estranged from them and is now in supported lodgings. She is not an offender, but has an ambivalent relationship with drugs and with support. (LAC non-offender)

3. Children who came into care in the teenage years, who had already committed offences and some of whom had also experienced maltreatment.

Fiona (18) was 15 years old when she came into care. She had experienced physical abuse and was aggressive and had already committed a range of offences. She combined great vulnerability with a potential to be violent. She had previously been in residential care and in a secure unit. However, her last offence was at age 16. She was currently well-supported in semi-independence. (LAC offender)

4. Children who came into care with multiple difficulties, but were currently well-supported and with some potential to cope.

Mark (17) came into care when he was 15 from an informal kinship care arrangement and had remained in residential care, where he was happy and well supported. He had learning difficulties and challenging behaviour. He was not an offender but was likely to struggle with the demands of independent living. (LAC non-offender)

Coping, with support: trust in relationships

The availability of relationships with adults or peers who can be trusted is essential for all young people, especially young people in care. But for this group there was a sense that, compared to the more resilient group, uncertain personal resources made support particularly significant. What characterised this group, who were coping but with support, was that the support was less likely to be coming from parent figures and more likely, as these case examples above indicate, to be coming from residential staff, supported lodgings carers or key workers in semi-independent or hostel accommodation. Where this support was excellent, young people reported coping surprisingly well with day-to-day living.

Stories of relationships in residential care were very varied, but for some it had been a positive turning point. For this young person, who had learning difficulties and needed a great deal of support, it had provided a safe and supportive environment where he could trust in the availability of others:

I live in a residential area. It's quite a nice place. I've got a big room and the people I live with are really nice and the staff are very helpful in giving me advice and other things . . . I have heard of other children's homes where the staff cower in the corner and don't really bother with the children. But this place is fantastic for that. They like being with us, they respect us, we respect them, they are nice to us and it's generally nice members of staff. I enjoy it here. (17, male, LAC non-offender)

This young person had previously been cared for by an extended family member, and he was still able to turn to her for additional support.

For other young people, residential workers had seemed less trustworthy, if only because nothing was private, everything had to be recorded and shared:

There was no one there to talk to . . . it's like the people who worked in the care home, it's like everything you said got wrote down and all that, so you couldn't really talk to them. (18, female, LAC offender)

For other young people, the onset of offending in residential care seemed to have damaged their ability to trust other people and their trust in their own identity:

I moved into a children's home and that was the worst move I could ever have made. I'd never been in trouble with the police, but from that day I had 42 convictions, fighting, theft, putting a knife to someone's throat. (17, female, LAC offender)

Some young people talked of being so out of control that they needed the kind of safe place that a secure unit could provide:

Well, I was in there for ABH, because when I lived in the care home I was drinking a lot and drinking made me proper violent and I got drunk and beat someone up on the street for no reason at all and got caught for it and got six months DTO but only did three months. I didn't like it at first but after about two weeks it was alright. I wanted to do my full six months in there. (18, female, LAC offender)

For this young woman, the wish to complete the six months was, in part, coupled with the aim of completing some educational qualifications that had seemed to be more possible once she felt safe and controlled.

The accounts of the living arrangements and intensive support that was provided in certain areas for young people who had moved on to semi-independent living arrangements were impressive. The level of relationship-based support was clearly helping young people who had not previously felt able to trust in adults and was also encouraging them to feel more confidence in themselves. This 17-year-old had previously been in secure units following violent offences, but then moved into semi-independent living following a beneficial experience of residential care:

I'm not in, like, a care system living with other people, but I have my own house, and I have a lady who comes round and she really helps me out . . .

What sorts of things does she help you with?

Like cooking and stuff, just little things. Like if I am going to an interview or something she takes me, like gives me tips with money and goes over papers when they come to my door. And I have a worker called T and she's, like, not my social worker but my key worker. She takes me to my appointments, but some-times I have to make my appointments for myself so she's good, she comes to see me six hours a week. I never had a worker like that, but now I do think it's better. I think kids do need that. (17, female, LAC offender)

The key worker system for these young people seemed exceptional in providing the kind of cover and advice that could enable young people to feel more confident and able to cope, including a sense of 24-hour availability:

She [key worker] will be proper understanding . . . She's proper lovely, she does everything for me, she's always there for me. If I ring her at two o'clock in the morning and I need to speak to her, she's there for me. (17, female, LAC offender)

Linked to this availability and trust in support was the time and opportunity that workers provided to think together and solve problems. For these adolescents it was clear that they continued to need assistance in thinking things through, regulating their feelings, and solving problems. This 18-year-old in a semi-independent living arrangement, previously in a secure unit, talked of the role that her key worker played in helping her and caring about her:

Well, when I'm mad and I ring her at work and she'll sit there and say G calm down, we can do this about it and that about it and we can go and see this person, I think they actually do care. Whereas there are some people in the care system, they are in it for the money, they don't care, but [voluntary organisation], I think they are there because they do care and want to help people. (18, female, LAC offender)

The trust in the good intentions of the staff that supported them and their commitment and care for the young people as individuals applied also to certain social workers, YOT workers and other professionals. One young person said of her Connexions worker, 'She's nice – she wants the best for me.'

Many in this group found maintaining reliable friendships difficult. Some had become aware of the negative effect of anti-social peers and had distanced themselves from their former groups, leaving them isolated. Whereas those who tried to please friends sometimes ended up behaving in ways (e.g. taking drugs) that they did not want and which caused them emotional turmoil. However, there were examples of young people who had good friends to whom they could turn and trust:

> *I don't know, they are always there for me, like we're not back-stabbers you know, I don't know, they're just always there for me. They are a good influence when I was going through all this. They were trying to pull me out of it. They've always been there.* (17, female, LAC offender)

> *We have been through the same stuff and we've been in care and we have lived with each other so we know the ins and outs with each other.* (18, female, LAC offender)

Partners were rarely a good influence in this group and a number of young women had previously been or were currently in relationships that threatened their ability to make progress in their education or stay out of trouble:

> *I met a boyfriend, it all went wrong, that's where everything, you know, it turned to where it was before, bad.* (17, female, LAC offender)

One young woman believed that her commitment to her education and a different future was so strong that it could not be shaken by her relationship with a persistent offender. But for most it was difficult to maintain their sense of direction when boyfriends were going in and out of jail or dealing drugs. There were risks for young women, in particular, of sexual exploitation.

For this group a delicate balance needed to be maintained between playing safe and managing some of the risk factors of the past, and taking advantage of their current stability to explore new opportunities supported by more reliable relationships.

Coping, with support: managing feelings, mentalisation and moral reasoning

This group of young people were coping with their day-to-day lives, but struggled more with thinking about and regulating their feelings than the more resilient group. Nevertheless, they had or were acquiring in the later teenage years some capacity to reflect on the circumstances and causes of their behaviour, which may have been helping them to regulate their feelings, behaviour and moral choices:

I don't know, I was just an angry person when I was younger. I was just aggressive to everyone and anyone.

Do you think that was fuelled by anything?

I don't know. I've got ADHD, but that ain't like an excuse or anything. A lot of things made me angry. I'm a stubborn person and it made me angry and I am stubborn so I will stay angry, and when I realised I was getting away with it and getting excluded and nothing was happening, I just did it again and again and again. When I am in an argument, I want to make sure I win, so I made sure I won the arguments with the teachers even though I got excluded, so I didn't really win, but at the time I was doing it I thought I was winning. (18, female, LAC offender)

It is possible to hear in this account some of the more sophisticated thinking and reflection that an older teenager can show compared to a 15-year-old, which was the age she had been when she had started offending.

The impulse to violence also needed some explanation, as young people looked back with regret and some understanding:

I had this big thing, getting into trouble, wanting to beat people up, and I thought I only want to beat this person up because I want her to feel the pain that I felt. Then I went to jail and my foster carer didn't want me. (17, female, LAC offender)

As young people reflected on their offending, they were able to see how destructive or pointless their behaviour had been, but felt that a downward spiral had become inevitable at the time:

I don't know why I did it because every time I did a crime, I've been like on an order for the crime before, and what was going through my head was I'm not going to get caught but I got caught every time, I got caught most of the time, and I don't understand why I did it, and I got to a point where I just did not care if I went to jail and I ended up going. (18, female, LAC offender)

For some still vulnerable young people, there had been some kind of turning point that had made them stop and think. This young woman had a baby who had been placed for adoption and was now trying to move on, with support:

I didn't have nothing to care about. It was just me living in a children's home, no family, no boyfriend, no nothing. Then obviously, as I have got older, I have started seeing my family more and had a baby, you just grow up. I never thought I would . . . I have grown up. I don't go robbing people now. I don't need to . . . It doesn't pay. You sort yourself out one day, but it doesn't help. It won't help you get a job. I regret everything, me. I wish I went to school and didn't get arrested all the time. (18, female, LAC offender)

These reflections and regrets are about the impact of offending on her own life rather than the impact on other people, so her moral reasoning is perhaps limited.

Other young people in this group seemed to lack a moral sense, which suggested some risk of re-offending. One young person (15) had been in care for a year and settled well in a residential placement. He attended school and had not offended recently, but he lacked any sense of constraint on his behaviour on the basis of other people's feelings. For example, he talked of humiliating another boy when out with friends and described a violent incident with the police, which he saw as having been a game that ended in his arrest:

> *There was about eight of us, and thinking, right, police, we started throwing bottles, stones, we were just pelting them, we got blocked in as well, and they squished us.* (15, male, LAC offender)

Although his placement was keeping him out of the way of his anti-social peer group, it was not clear that he had modified his basic beliefs.

For some young people, there was a sense that, although they were able to regulate their feelings to some degree, this was achieved by refusing to reflect on the past and living very much in the present.

Coping, with support: self-esteem

Very often these older teenagers, who were coping and stable, were able to look back on a point in time, a turning point, when those who had been offending or into alcohol or drugs had realised that they needed to take some pride in themselves:

> *This one day when I was 14 I told myself, this can't happen anymore. I can't be doing these things. When I am older, I won't get no job. I looked at myself in the mirror and said to myself, I'm not ugly. I've got nice legs, nice shape, body, face. Why am I going to downgrade myself?* (17, female, LAC offender)

The experience of either being previously excluded from school or not having properly engaged with education meant that it took an effort to change and be different, but some people were proud of making the effort:

> *I think I have done alright, because I have walked out of lots of them [colleges] but I have stuck with this one. I think it's because I am at a point in my life where you either do it or you will end up nowhere.* (18, female, LAC offender)

What was helping to keep individuals in this group stable and engaged with society was constructive engagement in education, training and activities. This was providing a sense of direction and also a source of achievement:

> *I am starting a new course on Monday. It's the Prince's Trust so it's getting goals and working towards them.* (17, male, LAC non-offender)

For all the young people it was important not to have too much time on their hands and the need for routine activity led to busy schedules at times:

> *Right now I have turned 17 so I am living independently and I go to college on a Friday 12–2, Tuesday I do . . . Wednesday I do boxercise, that's in the morning, then, Thursday I do gym 10–12 and on a Friday I do . . . in the week I'm like, I'm out.* (17, female, LAC offender)

One young person, who had been excluded from college and then moved placement, was volunteering four days a week in a charity shop while waiting for a new college term to start. This work had started as part of a court order but he had carried on 'because it was a nice place to work'. But it was also a way of filling his time constructively.

It was usually the case that young people had been helped to get on the right road in relation to education by being told by a trusted worker of the risk of their current pathway – and being offered help to take a different route:

> *Everything, like convincing me to behave and telling me risks and that . . . she put me on the right track and that, sending me to college.* (17, female, LAC offender)

Coping, with support: feeling effective, self-efficacy

Self-efficacy and self-esteem are closely linked and for some young people, being determined to get on in college and proving people wrong fostered both a sense of pride and a determination that they could follow through on a plan and feel effective. But relationships were often important here. In this case, the young person felt she owed something to people who had tried to help her:

> Yeah, they put me on a violence register. I had, like, a piece of paper that any college I went to or anywhere I worked, it was like a risk assessment, nobody would want me. I got this college placement and they were the only people who believed in me and so I had to do something for them, you know. Like when someone does something for you that's proper genuine and you know that they shouldn't really have done it but they have, they've given you a trial, they've given you a chance . . . Before I would have been 'Oh f . . . off', but this time I have took it as a chance, to prove people wrong. Everyday I go. I haven't missed one appointment. I just go. I have to think to myself, even if it's half-seven, I think I have to do it, even if I stand in the shower with my eyes still closed, trust me, I have to do these things, because no one else is going to do it for me. (17, female, LAC offender)

For some young people, feeling effective was explicitly linked with being offered choices, for example, about college or courses. This young person had thought through career options that might be to her advantage:

> My Connexions worker, she gave me a few choices and I chose that one. In September I am looking to be an electrician so I am looking to get a course to do that in September. But until then I am looking for a course to keep me occupied, so I am not just doing nothing. (18, female, LAC offender)

Although, for many young people, moving into semi-independent living might have proved too challenging, there were several in a particularly well-supported scheme who felt that the expectations of being more independent had steadied them and made them take responsibility for their lives. Asked what had made the difference, this young woman commented:

I don't know, just having the responsibility to look after myself – before, when I was in foster care, I would run wild, now I have more independence, routine, I want to go somewhere in life. [Housing association] have been really good to me. (17, female, LAC offender)

For some young people in this group, who were less confident about their ability to be effective and get a firm grip on their lives, the role of alcohol, drugs and peer pressure was still a constant challenge:

You stay awake when you have college, then you go to college and you are so paranoid, your eyes go funny and you don't want to get addicted and you think if you don't do it your friend won't like you. It makes you feel all crabby, you feel like a druggie . . . it's horrible because I haven't done it in a while but it's just there, as in your friend's house and that you are like . . . if they start doing it you feel left out. There's quite a lot of peer pressure and it costs a lot. (17, female, LAC non-offender)

Such young people were coping, but lacked confidence in their ability to make decisions and follow them through if they then lost their peer group.

Coping, with support: belonging, identity and values

Many young people had complex family relationships with birth and/ or foster families, with a consequent effect on their sense of belonging. Few had uncomplicated relationships with birth or foster families and this could be linked with a number of aspects of their identity. In this young woman's case, it was her ethnicity:

This lady [foster mother] what I called mum and dad, they brought me up in a white environment. I didn't know my culture. I thought they were my mum and dad. I was thinking, why am I not white? I went to high school and started hanging with the wrong people and it was really, really good where I was living and it all went. She couldn't cope with me. (17, female, LAC offender)

After a long gap, however, which included multiple placements and escalating offending, she was able to settle and sort out her life, including reconnecting with these foster carers:

I have got in contact with the parents who looked after me till I was 12 and I have a good relationship with them now. (17, female, LAC offender)

This pattern of returning to disrupted relationships when the dust has settled and the young person is able to resolve some of their feelings has been reported previously in foster care (Schofield, 2003) and adoption (Howe, 1996). So it is important for foster carers and adoptive parents – and residential workers – to keep the doors open for young people who may be able to reconnect with them.

One of the reasons for more complicated family relationships in this group were the often unresolved feelings towards parents regarding the reasons for being in care. This young person came into care when she was less than two years old. She had little contact with her mother until she was in her teens, when the contact contributed to a downward spiral into offending:

The thing with my birth mum is she can't come to terms with it. I don't hate her or blame her because she brought me into this world, she could have had an abortion . . . she brought me into this world so I have to thank her for that. But I will always dislike her. (17, female, LAC offender)

One young person had been subject to long-term emotional and physical abuse by his father. The offences for which he was convicted were assaults on his father in his teenage years after he had unsuccessfully asked to be taken into care for his own protection. He had a history of depression and suicide attempts, but had become more settled in residential care. His feelings for his family were mixed, although he did continue to visit the family home regularly.

Where young people had relationships with birth relatives who were pro-social, this gave them the chance to connect with a family member who was not delinquent or on drugs, as other family members were. One 17-year-old boy had experienced abuse by his parents, but he was able to visit frequently, his grandmother, who he described as 'the nicest person in the world', as she lived half-an-hour's walk away.

Also complicated were cases where young people had returned from care to live with parents; for them, other options were now closed. One boy had come into care at the age of eight following abuse and neglect from his parents who both had significant mental health problems. He had then experienced a stable eight-year foster placement with therapeutic support for his own difficulties, but could still describe the contrast:

> *I used to have to protect my dad. I used to have to stop him going into the kitchen to get knives and stuff . . . Living at my foster carers I managed to move on and realised I didn't have to do that.* (17, male, LAC non-offender)

It was unclear why this move back home had occurred, but he had since become angry and destructive in the family home and was distressed that he had lost his way and might also not be able to build on the educational progress he had achieved while in foster care. He did not feel he belonged anywhere and struggled with the idea that his foster carers were just doing a "job" that had come to an end:

> *It was alright, it was hard, well, for me more than her because it was her job at the end of the day. I found it hard realising this, it was like, I got so used to it that I thought she was like a member of the family in the end and I had to realise that she isn't and had to go back to my own family and get used to that.* (17, male, LAC non-offender)

There was something especially difficult for young people who had experienced the ending of a long-term foster care or adoption placement in adolescence. Being at home was clearly making this young person anxious, and when invited to think about his future, he said:

It isn't that I feel hopeless. It's like I don't know where to go and what to do sort of thing. (17, male, LAC non-offender)

It was a sign of sadness but perhaps also appropriate that some young people were able to acknowledge and describe rather movingly what it meant not to have a family at special times like birthdays:

I haven't had one birthday since I was 12 where I haven't known what my present was. For my 17th birthday this year I was really upset, got depressed and that, because it's sad. You've got your friends and that, but they're not your family. On their birthdays they see their mum and dad – and it gets to you. (17, female, LAC offender)

However, in cases where young people had resented their care identity, living in semi-independent accommodation felt like a step forward in just being themselves:

Why can't we stay at our friend's house? Why do we have to be reported missing? Things like this – why do we have to be put on welfare? Go to jail on welfare? Why do we have to have all these meetings and you decide what my life is? ... I feel so good in myself because I am out of that system. I am not in their hands ... I have [housing association] housing. I have my own housing. I'm doing good for myself. I haven't done owt, I get what I can out of social services. (17, female, LAC offender)

For many young people, as they moved towards establishing an identity for themselves, there were concerns that they might turn out like their parents, and with their parents' values and identity, especially where drugs had been the problem for the parent and were now a problem for the young person:

I feel dirty doing it. I am someone who I don't want to be. I am going to turn out like my mum so much I hate it. I actually detest drugs. I felt like do it and you feel like you are part of something and it makes you happy and then afterwards you feel like you are going to cry and you see things. I thought there was a man in my room with a knife. It's horrible. (16, female, LAC offender)

Vulnerable and high risk

For some young people, there existed a combination of vulnerability and high risk, with the risk being both in relation to offending and to mental health, separately and in combination. It is important when thinking about the links between mental health and offending to bear in mind the links between apparently different reactions to stress. Although traditionally there is said to be a divide between internalising and externalising disorders, especially in young people, it is not uncommon for there to be co-morbidity between, on the one hand, mood disorders, such as depression and anxiety, and on the other hand, conduct disorders and anti-social behaviour. Thus dangerous violence may co-exist with suicidal ideation. Vulnerability to stress, which can trigger impulsive aggression and/or depression, may be deep-rooted in a young person's history or may be a result of current circumstances, such as isolation and lack of support.

Other risk factors, in particular, drugs and alcohol, also play their part in triggering an inability to regulate feelings and behaviour. Previously maltreated adolescents who have not been able to resolve their past trauma also struggle to regulate their bodies, so eating, sleeping and sexual behaviour can be problematic. There is also genetic risk to bear in mind, with an inherited vulnerability to mental health problems potentially being triggered in adolescence. The few non-offenders in this group were vulnerable, in the sense, for example, of showing aggressive or impulsive behaviour, using drugs and/or being vulnerable to mental health problems.

It is important to differentiate between anti-social behaviour that is driven by underlying pathology arising, for example, from early trauma and sexual abuse, and that which is driven by sub-cultural norms that justify violence in relation to maintaining family or gang identity and reputation. But in many cases these overlap, with some young people who are unable to regulate their feelings and control

195

their impulses being drawn to anti-social peers and justifying violence in terms of external pressures and sub-cultural expectations. But offences were often serious in this group, including drug dealing, burglary, armed robbery and serious assault, and a number of young people had been in custody.

Vulnerable and high risk: pathways and case examples

1. Young people who may have come into care when under 10 years old or in adolescence, but have multiple problems that are unlikely to be resolved and which make a need for support into adult life almost inevitable.

John (17) came into care when he was nine. He was in a long-term foster placement, but became increasingly difficult to manage and moved into residential care. He had learning difficulties, behaviour problems (controlled with medication) and sexualised behaviour, and soiled when distressed. (LAC non-offender)

Peter (19) came into care at age 15 and found his residential placement supportive. But it seemed likely that the combination of learning difficulties, ADHD, epilepsy and multiple convictions for violent offences would mean that he would need ongoing residential support in adulthood. (LAC offender)

2. Young people who may have come into care when under the age of 10 or in adolescence, but who seemed to lack focus and direction and are drifting.

Will (16) came into care when he was two as a result of his mother's drug addiction. He lived in various foster homes, including a kinship care placement. He was currently in semi-independent living but drifting – not in education or training, smoking cannabis, being withdrawn, not able to reflect and unmotivated to change. Although he seemed a quiet, anxious person, he had committed multiple offences including GBH. (LAC offender)

Lorraine (16) came into care at 15 with a history of sexual abuse. There was evidence of sexual exploitation, self-harming and suicide attempts. She blamed her anti-social behaviour on alcohol, but found it hard to be motivated to change. (LAC offender)

3. Young people who were defiant regarding their impulsive violence and their entitlement to attack victims who "deserve it", including the police. This may be bravado, but appeared to have already led to quite serious offending.

Shelley (16) was adopted in infancy but became increasingly violent, including towards her adoptive parents, and came into care aged 15. She did not reflect on her aggression as a problem, but appeared to see it as a source of power and liked to shock by describing and justifying her behaviour. She expected to be loved and forgiven by family and friends. (LAC offender)

4. Young people who are likely to come into care late and are matter of fact or proud of their history of violence and offending because it links to sub-cultural norms – primarily peer group and gang-related, but may also be family-related.

Harry (17) came into care at 16. He had witnessed domestic violence. He had significant behavioural problems and was previously diagnosed as having a conduct disorder. He liked his residential placement and showed some motivation to change as he was now a father, but he still largely defined himself by his senior gang membership status and the value of his "rep" [reputation]. (LAC offender)

Vulnerable and high risk: trust in relationships

These young people were generally unresolved about their past experiences and found it difficult to think about or come to terms with their history of maltreatment and/or loss, and included asylum-seeking children. Some of this was due to the trauma of those histories, compounded by their own learning difficulties, mental health problems and ongoing contact, in some cases, with dysfunctional or rejecting birth families. Care histories were also stories of disruption, as their difficult behaviour caused and was then exacerbated by moves. For the young people who had experienced long-term fostering or adoption breakdown, there was a sense of a lost opportunity. There was sadness at the heart of even the most defiant young person:

> *I never really cared about anybody apart from myself, that was me when I was little. I didn't care about nobody . . . Because I didn't think anybody cared about me, I had been moved about so many times. It doesn't make you feel wanted, does it, being moved around?* (18, female, LAC offender)

> *I have good days and bad days, but it don't take much to send me off the rails. But people can go on and on at you about one thing and then you flip.* (17, male, LAC offender)

> *In Britain I tried to kill myself but to me, my small brother and my mum would come and say 'don't do that' [if they were here].* (17, male, LAC non-offender – unaccompanied asylum-seeker)

These young people talked about their relationships in a range of distorted ways that included a lack of engagement and trust in any relationships, or a preoccupation with relationships that focused on justification of their own aggressive behaviour. Some of this talk appeared to be bravado and may have been about shocking and impressing the researcher. But these seemed to be fairly consistent stories that young people told to themselves, and probably to others more generally, about anti-social behaviour being a necessary and often inevitable part of their lives, when other people could not be trusted. For some, violence was seen as a necessary part of showing that you cared enough to fight on behalf of a friend or partner or family member.

The young people in this group were currently living in residential care or some type of semi-independent living arrangement rather than in foster care, although most had been through foster care placements if they had come into care before the age of 14. Although some young people discussed selected members of staff positively, most of the young people seemed to have an apathetic or hostile relationship with them. They had an underlying view that staff did not really understand or were simply motivated by money rather than real feelings. Accounts of relationships, including with staff, often led to descriptions that focused on and justified their own aggressive behaviour – as in this account of an incident in a residential home:

> *I kicked a window in, no, two windows I think, kicked the car and went upstairs and got these heels on just to kick the car. They went upstairs and this worker was there and I have never liked her because she hates me and gave me glares and that and she started saying something and I just ended up punching her in the face . . . Everyone hated her, she was really rude to everyone, that's what she was, she was rude. Everyone was high fiving me when I came out [of police station]. (16, female, LAC offender)*

Beliefs about close relationships were also based on distortions that excused violence as forgivable:

> *I got nicked for assaulting my boyfriend – it's not a good idea, is it? And do you know what, my boyfriend took me back for it. I gave a break and I was proving that I am good and he took me back after I assaulted him. Proves how much he loves me, don't it? Because not many boyfriends do that. (16, female, LAC offender)*

Even relationships that appeared to be trusting did not seem to be having an effect on young people's violent behaviour. Accounts were given of being able to see family members whom they valued and who were genuinely supportive, but these relatives had also been the focus of their anger and aggression:

> *She [adoptive mother] takes me places, she takes me for dinner she takes me shopping, when she takes me shopping, oh my*

God . . . she buys me a lot, literally a lot. She's good. (16, female, LAC offender)

The young people showed no regret or understanding of the impact of their behaviour in these relationships or ability to learn from them in ways that might change their behaviour. In fact they often talked excitedly about their battles and expected to be loved and forgiven. They were likely to defend their sense of themselves as basically OK by a range of different narratives, though often revealing at times their sense of isolation and need for relationships.

Vulnerable and high risk: managing feelings, mentalisation and moral reasoning

In this Secure Base dimension, managing feelings, it was possible to see extremes that reflected different types of vulnerability. On the one hand, there were a number of young people who were unwilling or unable to think or talk about their feelings, behaviour or relationships at all, giving minimal responses to questions, but also being unable to engage in the hypothetical nature of the adolescent stories and speculate about the feelings of others.

For young people who did report on their experiences, it was often – as in the section above – about justifying their behaviour rather than showing any sense of being able to reflect on their own feelings or the feelings of others. Similarly, in the hypothetical adolescent stories, they would switch into their familiar aggressive response: e.g. 'I am going to smash his face in' or 'I will get my cousin to kick the living daylights out of him'.

Although some young people were able to reflect on aspects of their history with some understanding (e.g. one young woman reflected on her mother's schizophrenia), they were still not able to reflect on their own feelings and behaviour, often justifying their outbursts by blaming others or their own use of alcohol, for which they did not take responsibility. They often held to their story of how victims had provoked, and therefore deserved, their violence.

Not surprisingly, for more violent young people, moral reasoning involved a combination of justifications that suggested that what they did was acceptable:

> *If you hang around with the right people, the tough people, you don't care what you do because you're with the tough lot, you'll take anyone out who steps in your way.* (15, male, LAC offender)

> *There are loads of people who approve of someone hitting a police officer.* (17, female, LAC offender)

Some young people were explicit in suggesting that they would continue to offend and that the court process and the YOT were merely unwelcome interruptions – in this case, to earning income from dealing drugs:

> *If I wasn't doing YOTs I would probably carry on, because that was what I was doing, I was gaining from it, earning from it. Now I am not gaining nothing. I am having to sit around every couple of weeks doing YOTs and that, and if I don't do that then I will be getting breach and going back to court, so I'm not gaining from it now and not earning from it.* (15, male, LAC offender)

Though some talked of giving up certain kinds of offending, this was not based on any moral reasoning but was merely pragmatic:

> *If I didn't have enough money for food or alcohol, I would probably steal it . . . Do it when security are not looking. I don't do it anymore because there are plainclothes in there. If you are going to do it, do it early morning or at the end of the day . . . And when they are about to close, there's not that many people about.* (18, male, LAC offender)

Vulnerable and high risk: self-esteem
In the resilient and coping groups, engagement with education and activity was key to a more general engagement with society and also an attempt to build self-esteem. All of the more vulnerable and high-risk young people in this group had had poor experiences with school,

which included being bullied, low attendance, problems with peer and teacher relations and an inability to concentrate. These problems had affected motivation for returning to education. Many were not in any employment or education, some having been recently excluded through non-participation, and those that were in education did not appear motivated. Some young people spoke about not being able to get out of bed in the morning or of spending their days smoking cannabis. Most had few aspirations for the future and accepted fatalistically their current situation. Those who did have aspirations came across as vague and unconvinced with few concrete plans on how to achieve them.

One young woman was an exception to the unengaged profile of this group. She claimed to be focused on her education and enjoyed college because her ambition was to join the army, which she believed could help her with her aggression:

> Be the one with the gun. Be the one going to Afghanistan and that ... It will help me with my anger and that because you have to be focused. (16, female, LAC offender)

Young people were mostly drifting through their days, whether in residential care or semi-independent living, playing computer games, watching films and, for some, social networking. There was much talk of just "chilling". This lifestyle was managed very differently, with some young people seeming very flat, empty and hopeless, while others were engaged to some degree with other people and felt less isolated and more connected. However, where cannabis was a major part of young people's lives, it seemed to be both a contributory cause and a consequence of the lack of motivation to become engaged with opportunities on offer from their support workers. Drug use, particularly cannabis, is almost taken for granted by professionals working with young people and by the young people themselves. For some young people it had become a kind of habitual self-medication, but seemed, from their accounts, to be having a very deadening effect on their lives.

An area of self-esteem that was problematic from an offending point of view was the esteem associated with violence, even in residential care. As one young person put it:

When you're in a kid's home you have to prove you're hard, you have to prove you are big, just to get a rep. It's like on the street, you've got to earn your stripes. (17, male, LAC offender)

This young person was more thoughtful than others in some respects, enjoyed his residential home and said he wanted to get out of offending. However, he still took pride in his gang status and seemed to buy into the values of his gang:

When I got to K, they call me the general because, let me put it like this, I'm in a gang in K and I have a rep. I'm in one of the biggest firms in London, we call ourselves, we're not a gang, we're a firm. That's how I got my stripes. (17, male, LAC offender)

He described what this status and his gang responsibilities involved:

We went West End a couple of months ago. We had a big fight.

What happened as a result of that?

Two of my boys were put in hospital, with stab wounds.

What effect did that have on you?

We all got together and said we're going back West and we need to finish it once and for all, so we went down there to finish it. (17, male, LAC offender)

On this occasion, the dispute was resolved without further violence, but the acceptance of violence was part of an alternative moral code on which self-esteem depended. Some young people placed out of area, for example, described having to return to their home area at intervals to maintain their status.

Vulnerable and high risk: feeling effective, self-efficacy

Self-efficacy and the capacity to act autonomously and plan for the future also reflected the range of experiences in this group: those young people who were entirely passive and accepted their lives as they were; those who were drifting; and those who felt an excessive sense of their own power, often, as in the example of gang membership above, through intimidating others.

For some who were very passive and drifting, drugs again were sometimes a factor – though perhaps at times a cause and at times a consequence of lack of energy and hopefulness about the possibility of change:

> This is what the drug does to you, proper makes you so you're not with it. You're just sitting there and falling asleep and you're proper. It's alright but it's horrible, it's a proper dirty drug. I regret taking it in a way because it's just no good. That's what happens in life. (17, male, LAC offender)

For the group that appeared to feel omnipotent, feelings of power were paradoxically linked to a sense that their anger was inevitable and so, effectively, out of their control, as this young woman described:

> Like if they mention my girlfriend [at the LAC review], like they keep mentioning her name in poxy reviews and all this and I have already told them that if I see it then I will hurt them . . . Hopefully her name won't be mentioned in the review otherwise I'm going to get nicked. I don't want to get nicked, do I, because I've already been caught . . . and police came out to me and I just flung myself on the floor and there were five coppers trying to handcuff me and where I am so strong I kept going like that. (16, female, LAC offender)

This account was not unusual in dwelling on the young person's own strength and ability to intimidate. This 16-year-old may yet grow out of the sense of excitement and perhaps reputation that she gains from these incidents, as older teenagers in the sample appeared to have done. But currently her apparent sense of the "game" element in her use of aggression was still dominant, so it was difficult to know the extent to which she also at times felt frightened by being out of control.

Vulnerable and high risk: belonging, identity and values

For these young people, as for the other groups, there was a range of sources of belonging and identity. For those who had some connection with their birth, adoptive or foster carers, there was some possibility of identifying with pro-social role models, although for these young people the story was more likely to be about defying those values. Most young people aligned themselves more with anti-social birth families, or with anti-social peers, which left them detached from their foster care or adoptive families and more positive influences.

Anti-social family ties for young people who had come into care in adolescence complicated their sense of whether they had a problem with violence that should or could be dealt with, or whether it was just inevitable. In this case example, the use of "we" in describing his family seems to suggest that the young person accepted a shared identity, but also thought he needed to change:

I beat up a guy for lying to me. It was over a petty thing, but I didn't like how he lied to me . . . On my dad's side of the family how we deal with problems is we knock them the f . . . out, step-dad's side the same, mum's side, yeah. They don't agree with it, but it's like you need to curb your temper because it's my temper that gets me in trouble. (17, male, LAC offender)

The stories of their birth families were always difficult and rarely simple as sources of belonging or identity. This young woman came into care at the age of five. An attempt at return home ended rapidly when she assaulted her mother:

At first when I first got taken off of her, I used to miss her a lot and I used to cry when I had contacts, but not because I wanted to be with her but because I didn't want to leave. When I come to being about 12, they let me see her without social services and I ended up moving back in with her. I think it was about two days. I went to go and hit her and I got put straight back into care. We clashed. She has to get her own way and she has to, I don't know, same as my little sister, they're both not all there. (18, female, LAC offender)

Where young people had returned home, there was also often disappointment. This young man had come into care largely because of his father's mental health problems, and these were still a problem:

It's hard really because my dad is more distant and quiet than what he used to be – it's like he doesn't want to be with us, he talks daft and stuff and then he says he's going to walk out, he says this, he says that. (17, male, LAC non-offender)

Where anti-social friends or gangs had a strong hold on young people, they were described as like a family that looked after its members:

My firm's a family . . . Everyone just looks after each other, it's like if I had money one day, I sort my boys out, if I don't, they sort me out. (17, male, LAC offender)

One area of difficulty for all young people in care was to manage their care identity. Young people who were struggling to manage their lives constructively in other areas, found the stigma and negative expectations associated with care to be a problem in the community and in their own families:

I mean a lot of people associate me living here like I have problems that I can't cope with. Some people think because I am here I am mentally unstable. (16, female, LAC non-offender)

They expect you to mess up, like a lot of my family, because I ended up going into care, they think I am going to mess my life up and not get a job and that. (16, female, LAC offender)

Although it was possible for young people even in this group to see this negative expectation as a spur to proving people wrong, the absence of reliable relationships and family identities and difficulties in accepting help forced them back onto their limited, personal emotional and practical resources. Given these young people's histories, and in some cases genetic risk factors, such as learning difficulties and mental health vulnerabilities, it was not easy to defy negative expectations.

Summary

- The themes of risk and resilience that had been identified in the literature were used to provide an analytical framework for the interviews with the two sub-samples of young people in care, the LAC offender group (n = 33) and the LAC non-offender group (n = 32).
- Five interacting resilience dimensions from the Secure Base model were applied:
  - trust in relationships;
  - managing feelings, mentalisation and moral reasoning;
  - self-esteem;
  - feeling effective;
  - belonging, identity and values.
- Three broad groups of young people were identified:
  - resilient;
  - coping, with support;
  - vulnerable and high risk.
- Across the three groups it was possible to use the five dimensions to demonstrate how individual risk and resilience factors interact with factors in the family, peer group, community and professional systems.
- Thus, experience of maltreatment in early childhood that was followed by sensitive, secure base foster care could achieve good outcomes – ideally, when this was an early placement after admission to care, but possible even when this placement was reached after other unsuccessful placements.

- Late entry into care in adolescence has the greatest chance of success if it capitalises on the protective capacity of relationships and involvement in constructive activities for developing adolescent social competence and self-efficacy.
- The emphasis here is on resilience as a range of qualities and strengths that can be promoted, not only by caregivers in placements, but also by birth relatives, friends and a range of professionals, including social workers, YOT workers, teachers and activity leaders.
- In contrast, children from backgrounds of abuse and neglect, entering care at any age, who do not receive sensitive and committed care or who have emotional and behaviour problems that overwhelm carers' best efforts to help, need highly targeted therapeutic and educational support and guidance. If young people do not receive care that meets their needs or the necessary support and guidance from agencies, and are not able to regain a positive developmental and social trajectory before they reach adulthood, the prospects are likely to be bleak.
- Any stage in a child's life from pre-school to late adolescence provides a potential window of opportunity for change, but relationships will be key to helping children take these opportunities.

7 Conclusion: models of risk and resilience in care and offending pathways

The relationship between care and offending is complex. As the literature has suggested and this project has demonstrated, many factors will affect the pathway of any individual child. This conclusion therefore focuses on bringing these threads together to suggest the ways in which different factors at each stage can affect an individual pathway.

The first diagram (Figure 6) brings together the risk and protective factors that reflect both our review of the wider research literature and the findings from this study. No model can entirely capture the complex accumulation and interaction of different factors, but here we focus on risk and protective factors at each developmental stage.

The second diagram (Figure 7) shows potential pathways from abuse and neglect to offending. The emphasis here is on the significance of timely intervention and the role of high quality care in placements. It also suggests the increased significance of multi-agency involvement in working with adolescents in placement and when leaving care in order to mitigate the accumulated risk that comes from the impact of abuse and neglect through middle childhood and into adolescence.

Just as the child's difficulties spin out into education and the community, including through offending, so education and community services need to be available to create turning points that build positive relationships, provide opportunities for constructive activities, reduce risk and promote resilience right through to adulthood.

The care system has proved to be effective in providing good care to children from backgrounds of abuse and neglect, promoting security, resilience and pro-social values. However, prior to care most looked after children have experienced many of the risk factors, such as adverse parenting and abuse, that also lead to offending. Thus a correlation between care and offending is to a large extent a result of

Figure 6
Risk and protective factors at each developmental stage

Riskload pathway

Pre-birth →	0–3 yrs →	4–10 yrs →	11–15 yrs →	16–18 yrs
• Parent alcohol use • Parent drug use	• Possible genetic defects • Foetal alcohol syndrome • Physical abuse • Emotional abuse • Neglect • Negative parental influence • ADHD • Impulsiveness • Difficult temperament	• Physical abuse • Emotional abuse • Neglect • Negative parental influence • Conduct disorder • Oppositional defiant disorder • Anti-social behaviour • Negative peers • Truancy • Exclusion • Little positive activity	• Early age for first offence • Repeat offending • Drug/alcohol use • Truancy • Exclusion • Little positive activity • Delinquent peers	• Repeat offending • Drug/alcohol use • Chaotic lifestyle • Exclusion • Little positive activity • Delinquent peers • Minimal adult support

Protective interventions

Into care/adoption	Into care before 9 years	Create a routine	Ensure accommodation is stable	
Placed with sensitive caregivers	Good match into foster care	Engage with education	Provide adult mentor	
	Few placements (4 or less)	Address drug/alcohol use	Provide flexible education/training/ Employment opportunities with extra support	
	Long-term placements	Screen for mental health and SEN provide therapy/support		
		Provide opportunities for positive activity		

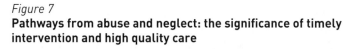

Figure 7
Pathways from abuse and neglect: the significance of timely intervention and high quality care

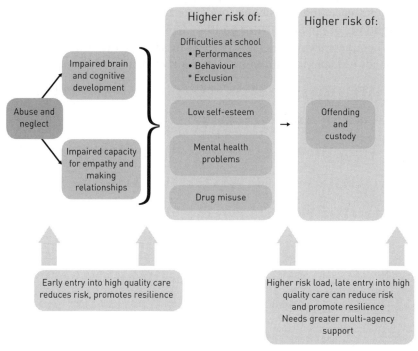

shared risk factors. Early entry to care followed by sensitive parenting in a stable placement with good professional support from a range of agencies, including education and health, minimises the risk of offending behaviour. Late entry into care in adolescence can also reduce the risk of offending if it capitalises on the protective potential of relationships and involvement in constructive activities.

However, if children in care from backgrounds of abuse have significant emotional and behavioural problems, do not have stable placements with sensitive caregivers and do not have appropriate professional support, they will be at risk of a range of poor outcomes, including being at risk of offending. An additional risk factor for looked after children is inappropriate criminalisation through police and court involvement as a response to challenging behaviour or minor offences in their placements.

Two of the most crucial periods are entry into care during adolescence and transitions from care to independence. These are windows of opportunity for positive change, but they also carry risk. When the system works effectively at these crucial turning points, it builds resilience and this must be the goal of all interventions.

References

Aber J. L., Brown, J. L. and Jones S. M. (2003) 'Developmental trajectories toward violence in middle childhood: course, demographic differences, and response to school-based intervention', *Developmental Psychology*, 39:2, pp. 324–348

Achenbach T. M. (1978) 'The child behaviour profile: I. Boys aged 6–11', *Journal of Consulting and Clinical Psychology*, 46, pp. 478–488

Ackerman B. P., D'Eramo K. S., Umylny L., Schultz D. and Izard C. E. (2001) 'Family structure and the externalizing behavior of children from economically disadvantaged families', *Journal of Family Psychology*, 15:2, pp. 288–300

Ackerman B. P., Izard C. E., Schoff K., Youngstrom E. A. and Kogos J. (1999) 'Contextual risk, caregiver emotionality, and the problem behaviors of six- and seven-year-old children from economically disadvantaged families', *Child Development*, 70, pp. 1415–1427

Ainsworth M. D. S., Bell S. and Stayton D. (1971) 'Individual differences in strange-situation behaviour of one-year-olds', in Schaffer H. (ed.) *The Origins of Human Social Relations*, New York: Academic Press

Allen R. (2011) *Last Resort? Exploring the reduction in child imprisonment 2008–2011*, London: Prison Reform Trust

Amato P. R. (2001) 'Children and divorce in the 1990s: an update of the Amato and Keith (1991) meta-analysis', *Journal of Family Psychology*, 15, pp. 355–370

American Psychiatric Association (APA) (1994) *Diagnostic and Statistical Manual of Mental Disorders* (4th ed.), Washington, DC

Appleyard K., Egeland B., Dulmen M. H. M., and Sroufe L. A. (2005) 'When more is not better: the role of cumulative risk in child behavior outcomes', *Journal of Child Psychology and Psychiatry* (formerly *Journal of Child Psychology and Psychiatry and Allied Disciplines*), 46:3, pp. 235–245

Averill J. R. (1980) 'A constructivist view of emotion', in Plutchik R. and Kellerman H. (eds) *Emotion: Theory, research and experience*, New York: Academic Press

Axelrod R. (1984) *The Evolution of Cooperation*, New York: Basic Books

Bannerjee M. (2003) 'Peeling the onion: a multilayered view of children's emotional development', in Hala S. (ed.) *The Development of Social Cognition*, Hove, East Sussex: Psychology Press

Baron-Cohen S. (1991) 'Precursors to a theory of mind: understanding attention in others', in Whiten A. (ed.) *Natural Theories of Mind: Evolution, development and simulation of everyday mindreading*, Oxford: Blackwell

Barter C. A. (2007) 'Prioritising young people's concerns in residential care: responding to peer violence', in Kendrick A (ed.) *Residential Child Care: Prospects and challenges (Research Highlights in Social Work Series, 47)*, London: Jessica Kingsley

Barth J. and Bastiani A. (1997) 'A longitudinal study of emotion recognition and preschool children's social behavior', *Merrill-Palmer Quarterly*, 43, pp. 107–128

Baumrind D. (1989) 'Rearing competent children', in Damon W. (ed.) *Child Development Today and Tomorrow*, San Francisco: Jossey-Bass

Bebbington A. and Miles J. (1989) 'The background of children who enter local authority care', *British Journal of Social Work*, 19:1, pp. 349–368

Beek M. and Schofield G. (2004) *Providing a Secure Base in Long-Term Foster Care*, London: BAAF

Berelowitz S. and Hibbert P. (2011) 'I think I must have been born bad' – emotional well-being and mental health of children and young people in the youth justice system, London: Office of the Children's Commissioner

Berridge D. (2007) 'Theory and explanation in child welfare: education and looked after children', *Child & Family Social Work*, 12, pp. 1–10

Berridge D. Biehal N., Lutman E., Henry L. and Palomares M. (2011a) *Raising the Bar? Evaluation of the social pedagogy pilot programme in residential children's homes*, London: Department for Education

Berridge D., Biehal N. and Henry L. (2011b) *Living in Children's Residential Homes*, University of Bristol/University of York

Biehal N., Ellison S. and Sinclair I. (2012) 'Intensive fostering: an independent evaluation of MTFC in an English setting', *Adoption & Fostering*, 36:1, pp. 13–26

Biehal N., Ellison S., Baker C. and Sinclair I. (2010) *Belonging and Permanence: Outcomes in long-term foster care and adoption*, London: BAAF

Blades R., Hart D., Lea J. and Willmott N. (2011) *Care – A stepping stone to custody? The views of children in care on the links between care, offending and custody*, London: Prison Reform Trust

Borum R. and Verhaagen D. (2006) *Assessing and Managing Violence Risk in Juveniles*, New York: The Guilford Press

Bottoms A. E. and Wiles P. (1997) 'Environmental criminology', in McGuire M., Morgan R. and Reiner R. (eds) *The Oxford Handbook of Criminology* (2nd ed.), Oxford: Clarendon

Bowlby J. (1969) *Attachment and Loss, Vol. 1: Attachment*, New York: Basic Books

Bowlby (1988) *A Secure Base: Parent–child attachment and healthy human development*, New York: Basic Books

Bradley R. H. and Corwyn R. F. (2002) 'Socioeconomic status and child development', *Annual Review of Psychology*, 53, pp. 371–399

Braithwaite J. (1989) *Crime, Shame and Reintegration*, Cambridge: Cambridge University Press

Brennan P. A., Hall J. and Bor W. (2003) 'Intergrating biological and social processes in relation to early-onset persistent aggression in boys and girls', *Developmental Psychology*, 39:2, pp. 309–323

Bronfenbrenner U. (1979) *The Ecology of Human Development: Experiments by nature and design*, London: Harvard University Press

Brown B. (2004) 'Adolescents' relationships with peers', in Lerner R. and Steinberg L. (eds) *Handbook of Adolescent Psychology* (2nd ed.), New York: Wiley

Brown R. and Cehajic S. (2008) 'Dealing with the past and facing the future: mediators of the effects of collective guilt and shame in Bosnia and Herzegovina', *European Journal of Social Psychology*, 38, pp. 669–684

Bryan K., Freer J. and Furlong C. (2007) 'Language and communication difficulties in juvenile offenders', *International Journal of Language and Communication Disorders*, 42:5, pp. 505–520

Buss D. M. (2000) 'The evolution of happiness', *American Psychologist*, 55, pp. 15–23

Cadoret R. J., Yates W. R., Troughton E., Woodworth G. and Stewart M. A. (1995) 'Genetic-environmental interaction in the genesis of aggressivity and conduct disorders', *Archives of General Psychiatry*, 52:11, pp. 916–924

Casey B. J., Getz S. and Galvan A. (2008). 'The adolescent brain', *Developmental Review*, 28:1, pp. 62–77

Christoffersen M. and DePanfilis D. (2009) 'Prevention of child abuse and neglect and improvements in child development', *Child Abuse Review*, 18, pp. 24–40

Cloninger C. R., Sigvardsson S., Bohman M. and van Knooring A. L. (1982) 'Predisposition to petty criminality in Swedish adoptees: II. Cross-fostering analyses of gene-environmental interactions', *Archives of General Psychiatry*, 39, pp. 1242–1247

Coleman J. C. (2011) *The Nature of Adolescence*, East Sussex: Routledge

Coleman J. C. and Hagell A. (2007) *Adolescence, Risk and Resilience: Against the odds*, Chichester: John Wiley & Sons

Compas B. E., Orosan P. G. and Grant K. E. (1993) 'Adolescent stress and coping: implications for psychopathology during adolescence', *Journal of Adolescence*, 16:3, pp. 331–349

Conduct Problems Prevention Research Group (1999) *Adolescent Stories*, from http://www.fasttrackproject.org/

Conduct Problems Prevention Research Group (2002) 'Predictor variables associated with positive Fast Track outcomes at the end of third grade', *Journal of Abnormal Child Psychology*, 30, pp. 37–52

Cottle C. C., Lee R. L. and Helibrun K. (2001) 'The prediction of criminal recidivism in juveniles: a meta-analysis', *Criminal Justice and Behavior*, 34, pp. 367–394

Crick N. and Dodge K. A. (1994) 'A review and reformulation of social information – processing mechanisms in children's social adjustment', *Psyhological Bulletin*, 115:1, pp. 74–101

Dadds M. R., Perry Y. and Hawes D. J. (2006) 'Attention to the eyes reverses fear-recognition deficits in child psychopathy', *British Journal of Psychiatry*, 189, pp. 280–281

Dahl A., Campos J. J. and Witherington D. C. (2011) 'Emotional action and communication in early moral development', *Emotion Review*, 3:2, pp. 147–157

Darker I., Ward H. and Caulfield L. (2008) 'An analysis of offending by young people looked after by local authorities', *Youth Justice*, 8:2, pp. 134–148

Davies P. T. and Windle M. (2001) 'Interparental discord and adolescent adjustment trajectories: the potentiating and protective role of interpersonal attributes', *Child Development*, 72:4, pp. 1163–1178

Dean J. and Hastings A. (2000) *Challenging Images: Housing estates, stigma and regeneration*, Bristol: Joseph Rowntree Foundation/The Policy Press

de Cubas M. M. and Field T. (1993) 'Children of methadone-dependent women: developmental outcomes', *American Journal of Orthopsychiatry*, 63:2, pp. 266–276

Denham S. A. and Bouril B. (1994) 'Preschoolers' affect and cognition about challenging peer situations', *Child Study Journal*, 24:1, pp. 1-21

Dent R. and Jowitt S. (2003) 'Homicide and serious sexual offences committed by children and young people: findings from the literature and a serious case review', *Journal of Sexual Aggression*, 9:2, pp. 85–96

Department for Children, Schools and Families (DCFS) (2007) *Care Matters: Time for change*, London: Stationery Office

Department for Children, Schools and Families (2010a) *The Children Act 1989 Guidance and Regulations, Volume 2: Care Planning, placement and case review*, London: Stationery Office

Department for Children, Schools and Families (2010b) *IRO Handbook: Statutory guidance for independent reviewing officers and local authorities on their functions in relation to case management and review for looked after children*, London: Stationery Office

Department for Children, Schools and Families (2010c) *Sufficiency: Statutory Guidance on securing sufficient accommodation for looked after children*, London: Stationery Office

Department for Education (DfE) (2010a) *Children Looked After in England (Including Adoption and Care Leavers) Year Ending 31 March 2010: Statistical first release (SFR 27/2010)*, London: Department for Education

Department for Education (2010b) *Outcomes for Children Looked After by Local Authorities in England, as at 31 March 2010: Statistical first release SFR 38/2010*, London: Department for Education

Department for Education (2011a) *Children Looked After by Local Authorities in England (Including Adoption and Care Leavers) Year ending March 2011*

Department for Education (2011b) *Munro Review of Child Protection: Final report – a child-centred system*, London: Stationery Office

Department for Education and Skills (DfES) (2007) *Care Matters: Time for change*, London: Stationery Office

Dicataldo F., Zaitchik M. C. and Provencher K. (2009) 'Youth violence: prevalence, etiology and treatment', in Andrade J. (ed.) *Handbook of Violence Risk Assessment and Treatment: New approaches for mental health professionals*, New York: Springer

Dodge K. A. (2006) 'Translational science in action: hostile attributional style and the development of aggresive behaviour problems', *Developmental Psychopathology*, 18:3, pp. 791–814

Dodge K. A. (1991) 'The structure and function of reactive and proactive aggression', in Pepler D. and Rubin K. (eds) *The Development and Treatment of Childhood Aggression*, Hillsdale, NJ: Erlbaum

Dodge K. A. and Petit G. S. (2003) 'A biopsychosocial model of the development of chronic conduct problems in adolescence', *Developmental Psychology*, 39:2, pp. 349–371

Dodge K. A., Laird R., Lochman J. E., Zelli A. and Conduct Problems Prevention Research Group (2002) 'Multidimensional latent-construct analysis of children's social information processing patterns: correlations with aggressive behavior problems', *Psychological Assessment*, 14, pp. 60–73

Dodge K. A., Petit G. S., Bates J. E. and Valente E. (1995) 'Social information-processing patterns partially mediate the effect of early physical abuse on later conduct problems', *Journal of Abnormal Psychology*, 104:4, pp. 632–643

Dodge K. A., Pettit G. S., McClaskey C. L. and Brown M. B. (1986) 'Social competence in children', *Monographs of the Society for Research in Child Development*, 51:2, pp. 1–85

Dugmore P. and Pickford J. with Angus S. (2006) *Youth Justice and Social Work*, Exeter: Learning Matters

Dunn L. M., Dunn D. M., Sewell J., Styles B., Brzyska B., Shamsan Y. and Burge B. (2009) *The British Picture Vocabulary Scale*, London: GL Assessment Limited

Eccles J. S., Barber B. L., Stone M. and Hunt J. (2003) 'Extracurricular activities and adolescent development', *Journal of Social Issues*, 59:4, pp. 865–889

Eisenberg N. (2005) 'Distinctions among various modes of empathy-related reactions: a matter of importance in humans', *Behavioral and Brain Sciences*, 25:1, pp. 33–34

Ekman P. (1992) 'An argument for basic emotions', *Cognition and Emotion*, 6, pp. 169–200

Elliott D. S., Huizinga D. and Menard S. (1989) *Multiple Problem Youth: Delinquency, drugs and mental health problems*, New York: Springer

Fairchild G., van Goozen S. H. M., Calder A. J., Stollery S. J. and Goodyer I. M. (2009) 'Deficits in facial expression recognition in male adolescents with early-onset or adolescence-onset conduct disorder', *Journal of Child Psychology and Psychiatry*, 50:5, pp. 627–636

Family Justice Review Panel (2011) *Family Justice Review: Final report*, London: Ministry of Justice, Department for Education and Welsh Government

Farrington D. P. (1978) 'The family background of aggressive youths', in Herson L., Benger M. and Shaffer D. (eds) *Aggression and Antisocial Behaviour in Childhood and Adolescence*, Oxford: Pergamon Press

Farrington D. P. (1991) 'Childhood aggression and adult violence: early precursors and later-life outcomes', in Pepler D. J. and Rubin K. H. (eds) *The Development and Treatment of Childhood Aggression*, Hillsdale, NJ: Lawrence Erlbaum

Farrington D. P. (1995) 'The development of offending and antisocial behaviour from childhood: key findings from the Cambridge study in delinquent development', *Journal of Child Psychology and Psychiatry*, 36, pp. 929–964

Feldman A. F. and Matjasko J. L. (2005) 'The role of school-based extra-curricular activities in adolescent development: a comprehensive review and future directions', *Review of Educational Research*, 75:2, pp. 159–210

Fisher P. A., Chamberlain P., and Leve L. D. (2009) 'Improving the lives of foster children through evidenced-based interventions', *Vulnerable Child Youth Studies*, 1:4(2), pp. 122–127

Flannery D. J., Williams L. L. and Vazsonyi A. T. (1999) 'Who they are with and what they are doing? Delinquent behavior, substance use, and early adolescents' after-school time', *American Journal of Orthopsychiatry*, 69:2, pp. 247–253

Fonagy P. (2003) 'Towards a developmental understanding of violence', *The British Journal of Psychiatry*, 183, pp. 190–192

Fonagy P., Gergely G., Jurist E. and Target M. (2002) *Affect Regulation, Mentalization, and the Development of Self*, New York: Other Press

Francis B. and Soothill K. and Liu J. (2007) *Assessing Changes in Offending Behaiour in a National Cohort: An application of latent transition analysis*, American Society of Criminology Annual Meeting, 14–17 November, Atlanta (unpublished)

Francis B., Soothill K. and Piquero A. R. (2007) 'Estimation issues and generational changes in modeling criminal career length', *Crime & Delinquency*, 53:1, pp. 84–105

Franzen E., Vinnerljung B. and Hjern A. (2008) 'The epidemiology of out-of-home care for children and youth: A national cohort study', *British Journal of Social Work*, 38, pp. 1043–1059

Frick P. J. and Marsee M. A. (2006) 'Psychopathy and developmental pathways to antisocial behavior in youth', in Patrick C. J. (ed.), *Handbook of Psychopathy*, New York: The Guilford Press

Frith U. and Frith C. (2001) 'The biological basis of social interaction', *Current Directions in Psychological Science*, 10:5, pp. 151–155

Furstenberg J. F. F., Brooks-Gunn J. and Morgan S. P. (1987) 'Adolescent mothers and their children in later life', *Family Planning Perspectives*, 19:4, pp. 142–151

Gill K. L. and Calkins S. D. (2003) 'Do aggressive/destructive toddlers lack concern for others? Behavioral and physiological indicators of empathic responding in two-year-old children', *Development and Psychopathology*, 15, pp. 55–71

Gilligan R. (2000) 'Adversity, resilience and young people: the protective value of positive school and spare time experiences', *Children & Society*, 14, pp. 37–47

Gilligan R. (2009) *Promoting Resilience*, London: BAAF

Godwin J. and Maumary A. (2004) *Adolescent Stories (Fast Track Project Technical Report)* (electronic version), available at: www.fasttrackproject.org/

Goodman R., Meltzer H. and Bailey V. (1998) 'The Strengths and Difficulties Questionnaire: a pilot study on the validity of the self-report version', *European Child and Adolescent Psychiatry*, 7, pp. 125–130

Grogan-Kaylor A., Ruffolo M., Ortega R. and Clarke J. (2008) 'Behaviors of youth involved in the child welfare system', *Child Abuse and Neglect*, 32, pp. 35–49

Gross J. J. and Thompson R. (2007) 'Emotion regulation: conceptual foundations', in Gross J. J. (ed.) *Handbook of Emotion Regulation*, New York: The Guilford Press

Guglani S., Rushton A. and Ford T. (2008) 'Mental health and educational difficulties in children in contact with children's social services', *Child & Family Social Work*, 13, pp. 188–196

Hagell A. (2003) *Quality Protects Research Briefing No 8: Understanding and challenging youth offending*, London: Department of Health

Harris P. L. and Saarni C. (1989) 'Children's understanding of emotion: an introduction', in Saarni C. and Harris P. L. (eds) *Children's Understanding of Emotion*, Cambridge: Cambridge University Press

Hauser S., Allen J. and Golden E. (2006) *Out of the Woods: Tales of resilient teens*, Cambridge, MA: Harvard University Press

Hawkes C., Jenkins J. A. and Vizard E. (1997) 'Roots of sexual violence in children and adolescents', in Varma V. (ed.) *Violence in Children and Adolescents*, London: Jessica Kingsley

Hawkins J. D., Catalano R. F. and Miller J. Y. (1992) 'Risk and protective factors for alcohol and other drug problems in adolescence and early adulthood: implications for substance abuse prevention', *Psychological Bulletin*, 112:1, pp. 64–105

Hayden C. (2010) 'Offending behaviour in care: is children's residential care a criminogenic environment?', *Child & Family Social Work*, 13:94, pp. 461–472

Hinshaw S. P. (1992) 'Externalizing behavior problems and academic underachievement in childhood and adolescence: causal relationships and underlying mechanisms', *Psychological Bulletin*, 111:1, pp. 127–155

HM Inspectorate of Prisons/YJB, (2009) *Children and Young people in Custody 2008-9: An analysis of the experiences of 15–18 year olds in prison*, London: HMIP

Home Office (2002) *Narrowing the Justice Gap: Framework*, London: Home Office

Hope T. (1996) 'Communities, crime and inequality in England and Wales', in Bennett T. (ed.) *Preventing Crime and Disorder: Targeting strategies and responsibilities*, Cambridge: Institute of Criminology

Howe D. (1996) *Adopters on Adoption*, London: BAAF

Howe D. (2005) *Child Abuse and Neglect: Attachment, development and intervention*, Basingstoke: Palgrave Macmillan

Howe D. (2011) *Attachment across the Lifecourse: A brief introduction*, Basingstoke: Palgrave Macmillan

Johnstone T. and Scherer K. R. (2000) 'Vocal communication of emotion', in Lewis M. and Haviland-Jones J. M. (eds) *Handbook of Emotions*, New York: The Guilford Press

Keltner D. and Ekman P. (2000) 'Facial expression of emotion', in Lewis M. and Haviland-Jones J. M. (eds) *Handbook of Emotions* (2nd ed.), New York: The Guilford Press

Keltner D., Haidt J. and Shiota M. (2006) 'Social functionalism and the evolution of emotions', in Schaller M., Simpson J. and Kenrick D. (eds) *Evolution and Social Psychology*, Hove, East Sussex: Psychology Press

Keysers C. and Gazzola V. (2006) 'Towards a unifying neural theory of social cognition', *Progress in Brain Research*, 156, pp. 379–401

Kohlberg L. (1981) *Essays on Moral Development, Vol. I: The philosophy of moral development*, San Francisco: Harper & Row

Laird R. D., Jordan K., Dodge K. A., Pettit G. S. and Bates J. E. (2001) 'Peer rejection in childhood, involvement with antisocial peers in early adolescence, and the development of externalizing problems', *Development and Psychopathology*, 13, pp. 337–354

Lane R. D. and Pollermann B. (2002) 'Complexity of emotion representations', in Barrett L. F. and Salovey P. (eds) *The Wisdom in Feeling: Psychological processes in emotional intelligence*, New York: The Guilford Press

Lane R. D. and Schwartz G. E. (1987) 'Levels of emotional awareness: a cognitive developmental theory and its application of psychopathology', *American Journal of Psychiatry*, 144, pp. 133–143

Laub J. H. and Sampson R. J. (2003) *Shared Beginnings, Divergent Lives: Delinquent boys to age 70*, Cambridge, MA: Harvard University Press

Lazarus R. S. and Folkman S. (1984) *Stress, Appraisal and Coping*, New York: Springer

LeDoux J. E. (1993) 'Emotional networks in the brain', in Lewis M. and Haviland J. M. (eds) *Handbook of Emotions*, New York: The Guilford Press

Leppänen J. M. (2011) 'Neural and developmental bases of the ability to recognize social signals of emotions', *Emotion Review*, 3:2, pp. 179–188

Leschied A., Chiodo D., Nowicki E. and Rodger S. (2008) 'Childhood predictors of adult criminality: a meta-analysis drawn from the prospective longitudinal literature', *Canadian Journal of Criminology and Criminal Justice*, 50:4, pp. 435–446

Lewis M. (2011) 'Inside and outside: the relation between emotional states and expressions', *Emotion Review*, 3:2, pp. 189–196

Lipsey M. W. and Derzon J. H. (1998) 'Predictors of violent or serious delinquency in adolescence and early adulthood: a synthesis of longitudinal research', in Loeber R. and Farrington D. P. (eds) *Serious and Violent Juvenile Offenders: Risk factors and successful interventions*, Thousand Oaks, CA: Sage Publications

Littlechild B. and Sender H. (2010) 'The introduction of restorative approaches in young people's residential units: a critical evaluation', University of Hertfordshire Centre for Community Research

Loeber R. and Farrington D. P. (1999) *Serious and Violent Juvenile Offenders: Risk factors and successful interventions* (1st ed.), Thousand Oaks, CA: Sage Publications

Loeber R. and Farrington D. P. (2000) 'Young children who commit crime: epidemiology, developmental origins, risk factors, early interventions and policy implications', *Development and Psychopathology*, 12, pp. 737–762

Losel F. and Bliesener T. (1994) 'Some high-risk adolescents do not develop conduct problems: a study of protective factors', *International Journal of Behavioral Development*, 17:4, pp. 753–777

MacLean P. D. (1990) *The Triune Brain in Evolution*, New York: Plenum Press

Maluccio A., Fein E. and Olmstead K. (1986) *Permanency Planning for Children*, London: Tavistock Publications

Mandler J. M. (1984) *Stories, Scripts, and Scenes: Aspects of Schema Theory*, Hillsdale, NJ: Erlbaum

Marshall T. (1999) *Restorative Justice: An overview*, London: Home Office

Masten A. S. (2001) 'Ordinary magic: resilience processes in development', *American Psychologist*, 56, pp. 227–238

Masten A. S. (2004) 'Regulatory processes, risk and resilience in adolescent development', *Annals of the New York Academy of Sciences*, 1021, pp. 310–319

Masten A. S., Best K. M. and Garmezy N. (1990) 'Resilience and development: contributions from the study of children who overcome adversity', *Development and Psychopathology*, 2, pp. 425–444

Mayer J. D., DiPaolo M. T. and Salovey P. (1990) 'Perceiving affective content in ambiguous visual stimuli: a component of emotional intelligence', *Journal of Personality Assessment*, 54, pp. 772–781

McAuley C. and Davis T. (2009) 'Emotional well-being and mental health of looked after children in England', *Child & Family Social Work*, 14, pp. 147–155

McFadyen-Ketchum S. A., Bates J. E., Dodge K. A. and Pettit G. S. (1996) 'Patterns of change in early child aggressive-disruptive behavior: gender differences in predictors from early coercive and affectionate mother–child interactions', *Child Development*, 67, pp. 2417–2433

Meltzer H., Gatward R. with Goodman R. and Ford T. (2000) *The Mental Health of Children and Adolescents in Great Britain*, London: Stationery Office

Miles D. R. and Carey G. (1997) 'Genetic and environmental architecture of human aggression', *Journal of Personality and Social Psychology*, 72, pp. 207–217

Ministry of Justice (2010a) *Youth Crime: Young people aged 10–17 receiving their first reprimand, warning or conviction, 2000–01 to 2009–10*, London: Ministry of Justice

Ministry of Justice (2010b) *Breaking the Cycle: Effective punishment, rehabilitation and sentencing of offenders*, London: Stationery Office

Ministry of Justice (2011) *Youth Justice Statistics 2009/10, England and Wales: Statistics bulletin*, London: Ministry of Justice/Youth Justice Board

Ministry of Justice and Department of Health (2011) *Government Response to the Office of the Children's Commissioner's Report: 'I think I must have been born bad' – emotional well-being and mental health of children and young people in the youth justice system*, Department of Health Gateway number 16856, London: Ministry of Justice

Moffitt T. E. (1993) 'Adolescence-limited and life course persistent anti-social behaviour: a developmental taxonomy', *Psychological Review*, 100:4, pp. 674–701

Moffitt T. E. (2006) 'Life-course persistent versus adolescent-limited antisocial behavior', in Cicchetti D. and Cohen D. J. (eds) *Developmental Psychopathology*, Vol. 3, New York: Wiley

Moffitt T. E. and Caspi A. (2001) 'Childhood predictors differentiate life-course persistent and adolescence-limited antisocial pathways among males and females', *Development and Psychopathology*, 13, pp. 355–375

Morash M. and Rucker L. (1989) 'An exploratory study of the connection of mother's age at childbearing to her children's delinquency in four data sets', *Crime and Delinquency*, 35:1, pp. 45-93

Mullin B. C. and Hinshaw S. P. (2007) 'Emotion regulation and externalising disorders in children and adolescents', in Gross J. J. (ed.) *Handbook of Emotion Regulation*, New York: The Guilford Press

Muncie J. and Hughes G. (2002) 'Modes of governance: political realities, criminalisation and resistance', in Muncie J., Hughes G. and McLaughlin E. (eds) *Youth justice: Critical readings*, London: Sage Publications

Munoz L. (2009) 'Callous-unemotional traits are related to combined deficits in recognizing afraid faces and body poses', *Journal of the American Academy of Child and Adolescent Psychiatry*, 48, pp. 554–561

Munro E., Lushey C., Ward H. and the National Care Advisory Service (NCAS) (2011) *Transitions from Care to Adulthood: Evaluation of the Right2BCared4Pilot*, Loughborough: Centre for Child and Family Research

Murray C. (2009) 'Typologies of young resisters and desisters', *Youth Justice*, 9:2, pp. 115–129

NACRO (2003) *Reducing Offending by Looked After Children: A good practice guide*, London: NACRO

NACRO (2005) *A Handbook on Reducing Offending by Looked After Children*, London: NACRO

Nagin D. S. and Tremblay R. E. (2001) 'Parental and early childhood predictors of persistent physical aggression in boys from kindergarten to high school', *Archives of General Psychiatry*, 58, pp. 389–394

Nelson J. R., Smith D. J. and Dodd J. (1990) 'The moral reasoning of juvenile delinquents: a meta-analysis', *Journal of Abnormal Child Psychology*, 18:3, pp. 231–239. doi: 10.1007/bf00916562

Nowicki S. and Duke M. (1994) 'Individual differences in the nonverbal communication of affect: the diagnostic analysis of nonverbal accuracy scale', *Journal of Nonverbal Behavior*, 18:1, pp. 9–35

Nucci L. and Weber E. K. (1995) 'Social interactions in the home and the development of young children's conceptions of the personal', *Child Development*, 66, pp. 1438–1452

Oately K. (2004) *Emotions: A brief history*, Oxford: Blackwell

Oately K. and Jenkins J. M. (1986) *Understanding Emotions*, Oxford: Blackwell

Olsson C. A., Bond L., Burns J. M., Vella-Brodrick D. A. and Sawyer S. M. (2003) 'Adolescent resilience: a concept analysis', *Journal of Adolescence*, 26:1, pp. 1–11

Osler A., Watling R. and Busher H. (2001) *Reasons for Exclusion from School*, London: Department for Education and Employment

Palmer E. J. (2003) 'An overview of the relationship between moral reasoning and offending', *Australian Psychologist*, 38, pp. 165–174

Paterson S. J., Heim S., Thomas Friedman J., Choudhury N. and Benasich A. A. (2006) 'Development of structure and function in the infant brain: implications for cognition, language and social behaviour', *Neuroscience and Biobehavioral Reviews*, 30:8, pp. 1087–1105

Patrick C. J. (2006) 'Back to the future: Cleckley as a guide to the next generation of psychopathy research', in Patrick C. J. (ed.) *Handbook of Psychopathy*, New York: The Guilford Press

Patterson G. R., Forgatch M. S., Yoeger K. L. and Stoolmiller M. (1998) 'Variables that initiate and maintain an early-onset trajectory for juvenile offending', *Development and Psychopathology*, 10:3, pp. 531–547

Perry B. D. (2001) 'The neurodevelopmental impact of violence in childhood', in Schetky D. and Benedek E. P. (eds) *Textbook of Child and Adolescent Forensic Psychiatry*, Washington, DC: American Psychiatric Press Inc.

Piaget J. (1932) *The Moral Judgment of the Child*, London: Kegan Paul, Trench, Trubner & Co

Piaget J. (1976) *The Grasp of Consciousness: Action and concept in the young child*, Cambridge, MA: Harvard University Press

Plutchik R. (1980) *Emotion: A psychobioevolutionary synthesis*, New York: Harper & Row

Plutchik R. (2001) 'The nature of emotions', *American Scientist*, 89:4, p. 344

Pollack S. D., Cicchetti D., Hornung K. and Reed A. (2000) 'Recognizing emotion in faces: developmental effects of child abuse and neglect', *Developmental Psychology*, 36:5, pp. 679–688

Potton E. (2010) 'Young people in the labour market', in Mellows-Facer A. (ed.) *Key Issues for the New Parliament 2010*, London: House of Commons Library Research

Pungello E. P., Kupersmidt J. B., Burchinal M. R. and Patterson C. J. (1996) 'Environmental risk factors and children's achievement from middle childhood to early adolescence', *Developmental Psychology*, 32, pp. 755–767

Riessman C. (2008) *Narrative Methods for the Human Sciences*, Thousand Oaks, CA: Sage Publications

Roberts W. and Strayer J. (1996) 'Empathy, emotional expressiveness and pro-social behavior', *Child Development*, 67:2, pp. 449–470

Roche D. (2006) 'Dimensions of restorative justice', *Journal of Social Issues*, 62:2, pp. 217–238

Roe S. and Ashe J. (2008) *Young People and Crime: Findings from the 2006 Offending, Crime and Justice Survey*, London: Home Office

Rutter M. (1987) 'Psychosocial resilience and protective mechanisms', *American Journal of Orthopsychiatry*, 57:3, pp. 316–331

Rutter M. (1999) 'Resilience concepts and findings: implications for family therapy', *Journal of Family Therapy*, 21, pp. 119–144

Rutter M. (2006) 'Implications of resilience concepts for scientific understanding', *Annals of the New York Academy of Sciences*, 1094, pp. 1–12

Rutter M. and Silberg J. (2002) 'Gene-environment interplay in relation to emotional and behavioral disturbance', *Annual Review of Psychology*, 53, pp. 463–490

Ryan J., Marshall J., Herz D. and Hernandez, P. (2008) 'Juvenile delinquency in child welfare: investigating group home effects', *Children and Youth Services Review*, 30, pp. 1088–1099

Ryan J. and Testa M. (2005) 'Child maltreatment and juvenile delinquency: investigating the role of placement and placement instability', *Children and Youth Services Review*, 27, pp. 227–249

Sameroff A. J., Bartko W. T., Baldwin A., Balwing C. and Seifer R. (1998) 'Family and social influences on the development of child competence', in Lewis M. and Feiring C. (eds), *Families, Risk, and Competence*, Mahwah, NJ: Erlbaum

Sampson R. J., Raudenbush S. and Earls F. (1997) 'Neighborhoods and violent crime: a multilevel study of collective efficacy', *Science*, 277, pp. 918–924

Sanger D. D., Moore-Brown B., Magnuson G. and Svoboda N. (2001) 'Prevalence of language problems among adolescent delinquents', *Communication Disorders Quarterly*, 23, pp. 17–26

Schofield G. (2003) *Part of the Family: Pathways through foster care*, London: BAAF

Schofield G. and Beek M. (2006) *Attachment Handbook for Foster Care and Adoption*, London: BAAF

Schofield G. and Beek M. (2009) 'Growing up in foster care: providing a secure base through adolescence', *Child & Family Social Work*, 14:3, pp. 255–266

Schofield G. and Beek M. (2014) *The Secure Base Model: Promoting attachment and resilience in foster care and adoption*, London: BAAF

Schofield G., Beek M. and Ward E. (2012) 'Part of the family: care planning for permanence in long-term foster care', *Children and Youth Services Review*, 34, pp. 244–253

Schofield G., Beek M. Ward E. and Sellick C. (2011) *Care Planning for Performance in Foster Care*, Final Report University of East Anglia

Schofield G., Moldestad B., Höjer I., Ward E., Skilbred D., Young J. and Havik T. (2010) 'Managing loss and a threatened identity: experiences of parents of children growing up in foster care, perspectives of social workers and implications for practice', *British Journal of Social Work*, 41:1, pp. 74–92

Schofield G. and Ward E. (2011) *Understanding and Working with Parents of Children in Long-term Foster Care*, London: Jessica Kingsley

Schore A. N. (2001) 'Effects of a secure attachment relationship on right brain development, affect regulation, and infant mental health', *Infant Mental Health Journal*, 22:1–2, pp. 7–66

Seigel D. (1999) *The Developing Mind: Toward a neurobiology of interpersonal experience*, New York: The Guilford Press

Simpson L. (2011) 'What makes ethnic group populations grow? Age structures and immigration', Centre for Diversity of Ethnicity, University of Manchester.

Sinclair I., Baker C., Lee J. and Gibbs I. (2007) *The Pursuit of Permanence: A study of the English child care system*, London: Jessica Kingsley

Sinclair J. J., Pettit G. S., Harrist A. W., Dodge K. A. and Bates J. E. (1994) 'Encounters with aggressive peers in early childhood: frequency, age differences, and correlates of risk for behaviour problems', *International Journal of Behavioural Development*, 17, pp. 675–696

Skardhamar T. (2009) 'Reconsidering the theory on adolescent limited and life course persistent anti-social behaviour', *British Journal of Criminology*, 49, pp. 863–878

Skuse D. (2003) 'Fear recognition and the neural basis of social cognition', *Child and Adolescent Mental Health*, 8:2, pp. 50–60

Social Exclusion Unit (2002) *Reducing Offending by Ex-prisoners*, London: SEU

Stein M. (2006) 'Research review: young people leaving care', *Child & Family Social Work*, 11, pp. 273–279

Stein M. (2009) 'Young people leaving care', in Schofield G. and Simmonds J. (eds) *The Child Placement Handbook: Policy, research and practice*, London: BAAF

Stein M. (2012) *Young People Leaving Care: Supporting pathways to adulthood*, London: Jessica Kingsley

Steinberg L. and Avenevoli S. (2000) 'The role of context in the development of psychopathology: a conceptual framework and some speculative propositions', *Child Development*, 71, pp. 66–74

Taylor C. (2006) *Young People in Care and Criminal Behaviour*, London: Jessica Kingsley

Thelen E. (2001) 'Dynamic mechanisms of change in early perceptual-motor development', in McClelland J. L. and Siegler R. S. (eds) *Mechanisms of Cognitive Development: Behavioral and neural perspectives*, Mahwah, NJ: Erlbaum

Thoburn J., Murdoch A and O'Brien A. (1986) *Permanence in Child Care*, Oxford: Blackwell

Turiel E. (1983) *The development of Social Knowledge: Morality and convention*, Cambridge: Cambridge University Press

Umbreit M. (1998) *Victim Sensitive Victim Offender Mediation Training Manual*, Washington, D.C.: U.S. Department of Justice, Office for Victims of Crime

United Nations Economic and Social Council (2002) *Basic Principles on the Use of Restorative Justice Programmes in Criminal Matters*, E/CN.15/2002/5. Add.1

Utting D., Bright J. and Henricson C. (1993) *Crime and the Family: Improving child-rearing and preventing delinquency*, London: Family Policy Studies Centre

Verrecchia P. J. (2009) 'Female delinquents and restorative justice', *Women and Criminal Justice*, 19:1, pp. 80–93

Wachtel T. (1999a) *Restoring Community in a Disconnected World*, adapted from *Restorative Justice in Everyday Life: Beyond the formal ritual*, a paper presented at the Reshaping Australian Institutions Conference: Restorative Justice and Civil Society, The Australian National University, Canberra, February 16–18, 1999

Wachtel T. (1999b) *SafeSanerSchools Restoring Community in a Disconnected World*, adapted from 'Restorative justice in everyday life: beyond the formal ritual', a paper presented at the Reshaping Australian Institutions Conference: Restorative Justice and Civil Society, the Australian National University, Canberra, February 16–18, 1999

Wallis P. with Aldington C. and Liebmann M. (2010) *What Have I Done? A victim empathy programme for young people*, Illustrated by Emily Wallis, London and Philadelphia: Jessica Kingsley

Widen S. C. and Russell J. A. (2007) 'A closer look at preschoolers' freely produced labels for facial expressions', *Developmental Psychology*, 39:1, pp. 114–128

Widom C. (1991) 'The role of placement experiences in mediating the criminal consequences of early childhood victimization', *American Journal of Orthopsychiatry*, 61:2, pp. 195–209

Widom C. and Maxfield G. (1996) *A Prospective Examination of Risk for Violence among Abused and Neglected Children*, Annals New York Academy of Sciences

Wiig J. K., Widom C. and Tuell J. A. (2003) *Understanding Child Maltreatment and Juvenile Delinquency: From research to effective program, practice and systemic solutions*, Washington, DC: Child Welfare of America Press

Wong S. C. P., Olver M. E. and Stockdale K. C. (2009) 'The utility of dynamic and static factors in risk assessment, prediction and treatment', in Andrade J. (ed.) *Handbook of Violence, Risk Assessment and Treatment: New approaches for mental health professionals*, New York: Springer

Youth Justice Board (2008) *Education, Training and Employment*, London: Youth Justice Board

Zahn-Waxler C., Radke-Yarrow M. and King R. A. (1979) 'Child rearing and children's pro-social initiations toward victims of distress', *Child Development*, 20, pp. 319–330

Zajonc R. B. (1980) 'Feeling and thinking: preferences need no inferences', *American Psychologist*, 35, pp. 151–175

Zehr H. (2002) *The Little Handbook on Restorative Justice*, Intercourse, PA: Good Books

Zehr H. and Mika H. (2002) 'Fundamental principles of restorative justice', in Zehr H. (ed.) *The Little Handbook on Restorative Justice*, Intercourse, PA: Good Books

Index

internalising disorders 53–4
interpretation of intent
  see attribution bias
interventions 113–20
  delay in outcomes 32–3
  timeliness 120
  by YOS 80–5
interviews, young people's groups
  129–34, 159–69

key workers, support provided
  183–4

LAC
  see looked after children (LAC)
language ability 150, 152
language development 39–40
LAs
  see local authorities (LAs)
learning difficulties
  conduct disorders and 57
  and offending 22
leaving care
  new initiatives 9–10
  offending risk 18
  preparation for 104–8
  transition to adulthood 120–4
legal framework, care system 6–12
legal status, LAC groups 143–4
leisure activities 152–3, 175
life course persistent offender 26– 28
linear effect, of risk 29
local authorities (LAs)
  as corporate parents 14–15
  data collection 69–70
  LAC procedural obligations
    6–12
  national survey questionnaires
    65–6
  performance targets 7

Local Safeguarding Children's
  Boards 7–8
looked after children (LAC) 129
  assessment and planning 71–7
  characteristics 16
  LAC non-offenders group
    legal status 143–4
    profiles 129–34
    risk and resilience factors
      134–43
  LAC offenders group 129–34
    legal status 143–4
    profiles 129–34
    risk and resilience factors
      134–43
  LAC reviews 10, 177
  voices of xiii
Looked After Children (LAC)
  care placements 92–113
  interagency working 124–5
  interventions 113–25
  national survey 65–6
  prevention of offending 77–92
  targets and strategies 67–70

mental health problems
  assessments 72, 75–6
  interventions 114–20
  offending risk 21–2, 195–6
  residential care and 98–9
  in study groups 135–43, 156
mentalisation 160
  coping with support 186–8
  vulnerable and high risk 200–1
  young people's narratives
    169–73
mind-mindedness
  development 44
  lack of 116
moral development 33–5

237

negative influences 153–4,
172–3, 191
in custody 27
in residential care 19–22
placement location and 93
positive influences 59–60,
153–4, 174–5
in residential care 99
study groups 157
turning points 36
peer relationships
adolescent limited offenders 27
in residential care 19–22, 105
risks and protective factors
57–8
self-rated perception 135, 137–8
permanence
literature search 16–18
options for 10
personal advisors, for care leavers
121
personal relationships, trust in
165–9
personality traits, in offender
typology 27
physical abuse (pre-care) 50–2,
60–2
placements
interventions into 114–16
risk reduction 92–113
see also foster care
placement location 93
data management 68–70
factors in 11
placement moves 145, 146–9
in adolescence 180
belonging in 192, 194
study groups 154, 155, 156
placement stability 145, 147–8
government concerns 6–12

value of 79, 93
placement type, for LAC 145,
146–7
police officers
in focus groups 66
intervention strategies 86–7
in residential care 87–92,
100–1
in schools 117
policy-making (government)
see government policy
policy-making (LAs), targets and
strategies 67–70
positive activities
self-efficacy in 174–5
study groups 157
practice, child care system 6–12
pre-sentence reports (PSRs) 76
prevention of offending 77–92
prisoners
see custody
private sector accommodation
112–13
pro-social behaviour
family support 193
moral development 34–5
self-rated 135, 137–8
study groups 156
proactive aggression 53
probability, in risk and protective
factors 25
professionals, relationship quality
17, 19, 22
prolific offenders 132–3
protective factors 135
interactions 209–12
study group 155, 158
see also resilience
psychological adjustment, self-rated
135, 136–8